The Simple Gospel

Edited by Hugh T. Kerr
Calvin's Institutes: A New Compend

The Simple Gospel

Reflections on Christian Faith

Hugh T. Kerr

Westminster/John Knox Press
Louisville, Kentucky

Unless otherwise identified, scripture quotations are from the Revised Standard Version of the Bible, copyrighted 1946, 1952, © 1971, 1973 by the Division of Christian Education of the National Council of the Churches of Christ in the U.S.A. and are used by permission.

Scripture quotations marked PHILLIPS are from *The New Testament in Modern English,* revised edition, translated by J. B. Phillips. © J. B. Phillips 1958, 1960, 1972. Used by permission of Macmillan Publishing Company.

The excerpt from "Four Quartets" is from *Collected Poems, 1909–1962,* by T. S. Eliot, copyright 1936 by Harcourt Brace Jovanovich, Inc., copyright © 1963, 1964 by T. S. Eliot. Reprinted by permission of Harcourt Brace Jovanovich, Inc., and Faber and Faber Ltd.

Book design by Ken Taylor

First edition

Published by Westminster/John Knox Press
Louisville, Kentucky

PRINTED IN THE UNITED STATES OF AMERICA
9 8 7 6 5 4 3 2 1

Library of Congress Cataloging-in-Publication Data

Kerr, Hugh T. (Hugh Thomson), 1909–
   The simple gospel / Hugh T. Kerr. — 1st ed.
        p.   cm.
   Includes bibliographical references and index.
   ISBN 0-664-25171-4

   1. Theology, Doctrinal—Popular works.   2. Christianity—20th century.
I. Title.
BT77.K35 1991
230—dc20   90-46521

—→✳ Contents ✳←—

Simple Gifts

'Tis the gift to be simple, 'tis the gift to be free,
  'Tis the gift to come down where we ought to be,
And when we find ourselves in the place just right,
  'Twill be in the valley of love and delight.

When true simplicity is gained,
  To bow and to bend we shan't be ashamed,
To turn, turn will be our delight
  Till by turning we come round right.

Shaker song

Preface

As one who has been studying, teaching, and writing about theology for more than fifty years, I still bristle somewhat when I'm asked, "Tell me, what *is* theology?" Beyond the inner circle of professional academics, theology has always had to justify its existence by explaining what it's all about.

Perhaps it is the theologians' fault that so many think of theology as a mysterious and impenetrable jungle of specialized jargon and abstract ideas. The truth is theology has often been exactly that. But it need not be. Some theologians, ancient and modern, enjoy considerable popularity, such as Francis of Assisi, Dietrich Bonhoeffer, Dorothy Day, Thomas Merton, Mother Teresa, and Martin Luther King, Jr.

"But these are not proper theologians," some will say. "When *we* hear the word 'theology,' we think of the complicated systems and arcane vocabulary of Aquinas, Calvin, Schleiermacher, Barth, Rahner, and Tillich."

Well, there are all kinds of theologians and all kinds of theologies. Some are highly structured, rational, and systematic, and some are more mystical, personal, and intuitive. Many of the topics that theology addresses require our best thought and deepest concentration. How can we conceive of God? If God is good, why is there evil? Can Jesus speak for God and be God for us? Is there forgiveness and the possibility of a new beginning? What is the meaning of life, and where are we to find it? Is there anything beyond death? These are simple questions to which no simple answers can be given.

But we misunderstand the function of theology if we expect it to give definitive and conclusive answers to all the perplexities and puzzles of life. Theology, if a brief definition can be ventured, is reflective interpretation of faith. It is not itself faith; it is not necessary for salvation; it is not everyone's idea of a fascinating subject for study. First comes faith, the gospel, and one's own most cherished religious convictions as well as one's doubts, anxieties, and questions. Whenever we reflect on these, we are theologizing—whether we know it or not.

Those who have some special investment in communicating the gospel, such as teachers, preachers, seminarians, writers, and scholars, have no other choice. We are admonished to love God and neighbor with all our mind, heart, and soul—in other words, with everything we have available. To make the good news known and alluring, we need the best we can summon.

Sometimes we can get lost in the intricacies of theological construction and forget that the simple gospel is something that little children can understand, if we learn how to tell it without talking down to them. C. S. Lewis once wrote, "If you can't turn your faith into the vernacular, then either you don't understand it or you don't believe it."

The essays in this little book are exercises in articulating some aspects of the simple gospel. The chapters are written out of long experience as a teacher of theology and as an editor of a quarterly theological journal. The intent is not to make theology simplistic or to glide over the inevitable difficulties and paradoxes of Christian truth. But sometimes, and ours may well be such a time, we need to be reminded of the basic and essential affirmations of Christian faith.

ONE

Simple, Not Simplistic

There is a difference between a simple statement such as "This is the day the Lord has made" and a simplistic platitude such as "Have a nice day." The one, though simple, proves on deeper reflection to be profound. The other, a tired cliché, evaporates into thin air the more it is examined.

There is always a need, especially in times of great confusion and intellectual perplexity, to risk making simple statements about faith and life while, at the same time, resisting the temptation to oversimplify. Ours is such a time, and it takes some resolve and persistence to affirm the simple gospel when many are ready to decry what they denigrate as reductionism.

I

In many ways, the Bible and the classic creeds of the Christian church are on the side of what we are calling the simple gospel. It is true that there are long arid stretches of biblical history, Levitical rules and regulations, arcane prophetic visions, texts that are linguistically inscrutable, and convoluted Pauline apologetics. Scholars can spend a lifetime trying to unravel such tangled threads, but others are content to grasp the biblical essentials.

To pick and choose the parts of the Bible that make sense to us, leaving the rest to others, is often derisively described as making one's own "canon within the canon." But it seems inevitable that most of us will gravitate toward the essential and the simple rather than toward the complex and unfathomable. Preachers, church school teachers, the very young, and the very old know this instinctively and live accordingly. As Vincent van

Gogh described his painting style in one of his letters to his brother Theo, "Exaggerate the essential; leave the rest vague."

There are many ways in which the essential message of the Bible can be epitomized in simple affirmations. "But let justice roll down like waters, and righteousness like an ever-flowing stream" (Amos 5:24) was the favorite text of Martin Luther King, Jr., and it summed up his faith and his civil rights cause. The minor prophet Micah made a major declaration in the simple prescription, "What does the Lord require of you but to do justice, and to love kindness, and to walk humbly with your God?" (Micah 6:8). Jesus conflated all the commandments into love of God and love of neighbor (Mark 12:29–31). Paul, who wrote extensively on faith, hope, and love dared to reduce them to a single proposition, "The greatest of these is love" (1 Cor. 13:13). We are wary, of course, of proof texting, and we must remember that any version of the simple gospel depends on the full gospel. The essence must be distilled out of the substance, and textual epigrams presuppose the whole of the biblical revelation.

Preachers and teachers prepare their sermons and lectures out of a considerable background of study, reflection, and personal experience. But the sermon, after all, is itself a selective statement of the gospel and not an attempt to cover the whole biblical or theological waterfront. A teacher's preparation for class, at whatever level, must necessarily be a digest of previous reading and research. An effective and moving sermon should exemplify the principle that less is more, and a classroom session that draws students into the center of the topic must not linger too long on comparative analysis or documentation.

There are inexorable pressures working against simple articulations of the gospel's message. Seminarians become thoroughly indoctrinated into an educational structure that allows little freedom or individual creativity. In seminaries and divinity schools, and even more so in graduate studies, the curriculum is set up with departmental requirements that the faculty thinks best for the student. The result is often a three-year lock-step progression from one level to another with very little freedom of choice. Beyond the content of their courses, students also learn that scholarship means multiple bibliographies and term papers with copious attributions and footnotes. Incentives for cutting through this tangle of academic undergrowth are few and far between. Seminarians are rewarded for well-researched, documented papers, not for attempts at summary or reflective meditations on the subject matter of their courses.

II

Let me mention two or three personal experiences on the side of making things simpler. During World War II, along with many colleges and universities in America, theological seminaries were involved in what was known as "the accelerated program." The general idea was to speed up graduation by utilizing summers and reducing vacation time. This meant that many students could graduate before being drafted or, for those seminaries committed to the training of chaplains for the U.S. Navy's V-12 unit, the time necessary for commissioning could be considerably shortened. This also meant that college students entering seminary could matriculate at virtually any time of the calendar year and so begin their studies within the curriculum structure wherever it happened to be at the time.

As one who was teaching the systematic theology courses during this wartime period, I vividly recall the panic that this accelerated program created among some faculty as well as among deans and admissions officers. In my case, the normal sequence of courses in theology began with the doctrine of God and revelation, followed in subsequent semesters with the doctrine of sin and salvation, the person of Jesus Christ, the work of the Holy Spirit, the church and the sacraments, and, finally, with eschatology and the last things.

In retelling, it all sounds rather cut and dried, but at the time the sequence made some progressive sense, and it was assumed that the structure itself would be noted and retained by seminarians. After all, the creeds of the church followed the same sequence as did many hymns in the classic tradition and, to some extent, the seasons of the Christian year.

But what happened to students who entered the program not at the beginning of the sequence but at the end or somewhere in the middle? What would it mean to *begin* theological study with eschatology, or church history with the Enlightenment, or Bible study with the pastoral epistles? Apparently, as I recall, it didn't make any difference at all. This interlude made an abiding impression on my later teaching and my growing resistance to the stranglehold of curriculum restrictions and prerequisites.

I was confirmed in this conviction, curiously enough, by Karl Barth, whose *Church Dogmatics* many regard as one of the last great summa structures. When Barth gave his Princeton lectures in 1962, later published as a very slim volume entitled *Evangelical Theology: An Introduction*, it was announced that he would receive questions from the audience if the questions were written out beforehand. One of my students said he wouldn't dare ask Karl Barth a question! It would be, he hinted, like tangling with Socrates. "Why not?" I said. "Ask him whether he thinks it makes any difference where you begin to study theology." To my alarm, after one of the lectures, Barth read the student's question aloud and replied in words to the effect that, no, it doesn't make any difference where you start so long as Jesus Christ is at the center. It was also at this time, by the way, when someone asked Barth to distill the essence of his magnum opus in a few words, that he replied, "Jesus loves me—this I know, for the Bible tells me so."

The second illustration stems from the first. In recent years and at the present time, I offer to seminarians a free elective with the somewhat cryptic title "Theology as Critical Insight." It is "free" in the sense that there are no prerequisites, so the class is a mixture of first-, second-, and third-year students, some master's candidates, international students just finding their way around, and a few special non-degree auditors. At first, I thought the experiment would be utter chaos, with seniors regarding first-year beginners with disdain. But nothing of the sort has transpired. I tell the class at the beginning that we will try to learn from one another and that we will accept in good faith anything that anyone wants to say on any subject. We move the regimented chairs around, we sometimes get up to examine a picture or object, and we try to hear and see the gospel in new and unconventional ways. The final term paper is meant to be a personal reverie on what counts as authentic faith, with a realistic forecast of where the student would like to be in the next five years. I don't pretend that this method, such as it is, would appeal to everyone, and some of my colleagues probably resent the fact that the course is not structured within the prescribed requirements.

The third illustration relates to a longtime editorial supervision of the religious quarterly *Theology Today*. Since the first issue in April 1944, we have tried to define the journal's purpose as a scholarly but not pedantic or "guild" forum for articles designed for teachers and professors as well as pastors and ministers. From its modest start, *Theology Today* is now recognized as one of the foremost religious quarterlies in the world, respected not only for the high quality of its articles but for its concern to help the church and the ministry "keep theological." I mention this dual approach not in the interest of immodest promotion but to suggest that the journal's purview— articles of theological substance not only for professors but for pastors—creates some difficult editorial problems.

In recent years, it has become increasingly difficult to secure articles written in simple, clear prose, without too many cluttering footnotes, and with a single significant thesis set forth and developed in the space available. The current tendency in theological writing is to advance an analytical comparison of several people, ancient or modern, recognized in some sense as important and authoritative. Such writing comes across as mostly derivative, obscuring the views, if any, of the writer of the essay by attributing even commonplace statements to someone or some book considered significant. Most unsolicited manuscripts of this kind must be rejected simply because all we learn from reading these pages is what the author thinks other thinkers think.

There are obvious reasons why this convoluted comparative style has become so typical of theological writing. For one thing, this style is the generally prescribed methodology of graduate studies, and the prerequisite "credit card" for a master's or doctor's dissertation. The big, bulky *Chicago Manual of Style*, with its elaborate apparatus for footnotes and other notations, has long dominated the field of academic writing. That is certainly not all bad, but, from an editor's perspective, the methodology often seems to get in the way of what the writer has to say.

Another reason for the proliferation of footnotes and all the other trademarks of a scholarly paper is the availability, through library computers and other retrieval devices, of a vast world of literature that can easily be tapped and put to use in the bibliography and elsewhere. The writer need not consult all this resource material, but much of it can spill over into the manuscript by way of casual references and footnotes. A telltale giveaway of this possibility appears in notes that begin with "Cf. Bultmann's notion that . . ." or "On the history of this controversy, see . . ." or "For a fuller account of Augustine's views on sin and salvation, consult . . . ."

Editors and publishers are always trying to clarify what authors write, and this often means cutting off the first few pages, breaking up the long paragraphs, and simplifying the sentence style. Saxe Commins, a former editor at Random House, liked to describe himself as being in "the cleaning and repair business."

III

If now we return to the matter of the simple gospel, there is no one definition that could satisfy everyone. But that is part of the virtue of the phrase—it can be expressed in almost endless ways. The good news of the gospel, as Søren Kierkegaard saw it in his favorite text, is that "every perfect gift is from above" (James 1:17). James? Martin Luther's "epistle of straw"? How about this, from the same epistle: "Religion that is pure and undefiled before God . . . is this: to visit orphans and widows in their affliction" (James 1:27)? Emil Brunner once said that "Jesus is what God has to say to us." Harnack declared that "the gospel is something so simple, something that speaks to us with so much power, that it cannot easily be mistaken." For John Newton, the onetime slave ship captain, it was simply "amazing grace."

Some definitions of the simple gospel come to us not in words but personified in lives made luminous by the grace of God in Jesus Christ, such as Francis of Assisi, Julian of Norwich, Father Damien, Albert Schweitzer, and Dorothy Day. For others, we identify their lives with their words, as when Dietrich Bonhoeffer wrote from a Nazi prison that we should "throw ourselves utterly in the arms of God . . . and watch with Christ in Gethsemane." When Mother Teresa was asked if she thought working with the poor was the way to find God, she replied,

"Because we cannot see Christ [in the flesh], we cannot express our love to him; but our neighbors we can always see, and we can do to them what, if we saw him, we would like to do to Christ. . . . In the slums, in the broken human body, in children, we see Christ, and we touch him."

There is in every age an urge to simplify what has become too complicated or, similarly, to return to those elemental sources of power and creativity that we associate with vitality and regeneration. This quest for the original fountains of life goes hand in hand today with the search for a simpler life-style in the midst of an oppressive culture of consumerism. Environmentalists who want to keep forests and protected areas of land in their simple, natural state must constantly fight against individual and residential development. Nutritionists who look for simple products with fewer flavor enhancers or chemical additives have to resist the allurements of advertising and competitive ratings. Parents who look for schools where children can learn basic elementary skills are often frustrated by an impersonal school system and, in our inner cities, by a system out of control. We would like to discover simpler solutions for the problems of medical and hospital care, especially for our aging population, as everything becomes more technical and expensive.

IV

The obvious criticism of all attempts to articulate the simple gospel, or the simple anything for that matter, revolves around the charge that all such efforts result in oversimplified reductionism. Such critics remind us, properly, that life *is* complicated, that it is impossible to turn the clock of time back to some simpler age (if ever there was one), and that with all the failures and inadequacies of contemporary technological culture much good has been achieved and should not be ignored. No one wants to go back to the horse and buggy, the village doctor, the red-brick schoolhouse, the coal grate, and the kerosene lamp. So far as theology goes, great gains in understanding the Bible have issued from advanced and highly specialized scholarship, from archaeology, from the sociology of knowledge, and from new insights derived from cross-cultural awareness of other religions. Theological libraries are crammed with a vast variety of religious resources, and students and ministers now enjoy the luxury of a wider selection of texts than ever before. Special seminars, continuing education and higher degree programs, conferences, and summer institutes are commonplace and provide insight into new fields of religious life and thought.

If the great system builders of the ancient and more recent past have left few successors, we have today a richer variety of theological options and a radical questioning of previous presuppositions that make for a new kind of theological excitement. In the midst of this diverse and burgeoning situation, pleas on behalf of the simple gospel would be interpreted by many as a backward step and an escapist retreat from reality. To simplify would be for many to nullify.

A more incisive critique of the simple gospel charges that all reductionist efforts yearn, perhaps unconsciously, for a golden age of a pristine paradise where men and women live in innocent, symbiotic association with the animal kingdom and the un-spoiled world of nature. Thus, in this model, the church of the New Testament and early apostolic times, the original kerygma with a few major emphases, and the centrality of the Christ figure as norm for belief and behavior—these become the criteria of the authentic Christian gospel, and they must be identified and claimed by returning to the earliest gospel age. Once again, the simple gospel theme would appear to be withdrawal from our own times in favor of some mythical early age of innocence.

The history of church reform movements seems to confirm this critique. The Protestant Reformation appealed to the basic authority of scripture and the earliest creeds of the church. Subsequent Protestant denominational developments often designated as "the scandal of Protestantism" as well as independent and separatist sects and cults all laid claim to the original gospel as they understood it, and this usually meant abandoning accumulated liturgical and theological baggage in favor of the simple gospel. Roman Catholicism and Eastern Orthodoxy base their theological and ecclesiastical authority upon what they regard as authentic early ties to apostolic Christianity, thus making reform movements within these traditions suspect and unacceptable.

There is a considerable body of literature on this primitivistic tendency among the churches, stretching from *Primitivism and*

Related Ideas in Antiquity (1935), by Arthur O. Lovejoy and George Boas, through the writings of Sidney Mead and others, to Theodore Dwight Bozeman's *To Live Ancient Lives: The Primitivist Dimension in Puritanism* (1988) and Richard T. Hughes and C. Leonard Allen's *Illusions of Innocence: Protestant Primitivism in America, 1630–1875* (1988). Reporting on this analysis, with which he essentially agrees, Martin E. Marty (*The Christian Century,* June 7–14, 1989) thinks this primordium quest is what Mircea Eliade invoked in his numerous discussions of ancient myths and rituals. But surely this is a simplistic reading of what Eliade variously called "the myth of the eternal return," "regeneration through return to the time of origins," "the restoration of mythical time," or "the repetition of the cosmogony."

The reason for going back to primitive beginnings is not to find a shelter or sanctuary from what Reinhold Niebuhr liked to call "the vicissitudes of life." The lure of original creation-time, that primordial moment when cosmos emerged out of chaos, like the spirit brooding over the preformal waters (Gen. 1:2), rests upon the expectation that the original creative energies of *illud tempus* can be recovered and made dynamic for today and tomorrow. *In illo tempore,* as Eliade liked to designate creation-time, is translated into secular and sacred sacraments and ceremonies that celebrate rebirth and renewal. The primitive creative forces associated with Genesis or with the earliest apostolic faith provide a reservoir of regeneration, so that a *retreat* to the simple, essential, primitive creative beginnings is necessary to *return* to the present with a fresh vision for tomorrow.

In the Gospel accounts of the Transfiguration (Matt. 17:1–13; Mark 9:2–13; Luke 9:28–36), the evangelists no doubt wish to portray Jesus as the fulfillment of the law (Moses) and the prophets (Elijah); we may suggest this effort is a good example of primitivism or going back to the primordial beginnings. But Jesus rejects Peter's suggestion that three tents or shelters be constructed on the spot in order to prolong and perpetuate the mystical vision.

There is no way to live forever on that ecstatic Mount, and the evangelists all report that Jesus and the three disciples "came

down to earth." And the first reality they encountered was a
tormented child whom Jesus straightway healed. That, in a
biblical nutshell, is what it means to go back to the creative
beginnings to find re-creative vision for today.

And that is what we mean by risking to affirm the simple
gospel.

TWO

Everyone Begins Somewhere

When things got a little complicated in the Garden of Eden, God came in the cool of the evening and inquired of Adam, "Where are you?" (Gen. 3:9). The question was, of course, more existential than geographical, because wherever they were, Adam and Eve were in transit. "Where are you?" is a haunting question we need to ask ourselves periodically because it forces us to reflect on where we've been and where we're going. And it is a question of peculiar urgency for students and seminarians as well as for preachers and ministers.

I

In the older, conventional pattern of things, seminarians arrived directly from college to pursue a three-year course that included some additional field work, or internship. Then they graduated to be called, usually, to small, struggling congregations or as assistants or associates in larger parishes. That pattern still remains, but in recent years it has undergone significant change, affecting both theological education and parish ministry, a change also reflected in our colleges.

In a 1988 College Board report, "How Americans in Transition Study for College Credit," it is noted that about 45 percent of current college enrollments are for students *over* twenty-three years of age, with many still-older second-career men and women. The number of such older college students has more than doubled since a 1970 College Board report. At Harvard University, there are more than 55,000 older students enrolled in all kinds of continuing education and extension programs. This represents, as one of the Harvard deans observed, an "academic revolution in our midst."

What is happening at the college level finds its parallel in seminaries and divinity schools. The number of seminarians in their early twenties just out of college is decreasing, but total enrollments stay about the same because of the great influx of older and second-career students. This current development comes on the heels of the recent surge of the number of women in seminaries, most of whom begin with parish ministry as a strong vocational goal. The previously homogeneous character of a typical Protestant seminary campus no longer exists, and this clearly poses unprecedented problems for students, faculty, and, eventually, for churches and congregations.

The seminary campus increasingly reflects our pluralistic society; today's seminary is no longer a compact residential community whose students are more or less the same age and share the same educational background and the same cultural heritage. The younger college graduate, who has majored in history or philosophy, can move easily into church history or philosophy of religion or theology in seminary, so it has been assumed. But what about the second-career student who has been in banking or biology or homemaking for fifteen years and has decided on a new life-style of Christian ministry? And what about the growing number of third-world students pursuing higher degree programs who bring with them very diverse cultural, linguistic, and religious trends?

Seminaries and faculties are mostly ill-equipped to cope with this academic revolution. Attempts are made to set up a Black Studies Program, a Feminist Center, an Association of International Students, and the like. But this, in many ways, only draws attention to the diffuse character of our contemporary student population. In the meantime, the core requirements for a theological degree remain much the same, with little or no awareness of what this new diversity implies for teaching, assignments, bibliographies, writing, speaking, research, and the arts and skills of preaching and pastoral care.

The aging of new seminary enrollments corresponds to the aging of church congregations. In recent years within mainline denominations, congregations have been growing older, as has the general population itself. Sunday schools and youth groups are not flourishing, and changing neighborhoods tend to break up older, cohesive cultural patterns. It remains to be seen whether older seminary graduates will be welcome among older congregations. It might seem that the correlation is providential. Vacant churches that once looked for younger pastors to work with young people may in the future find in second-career graduates business management experience and special training in pastoral care, emphasizing ministry to retirement communities and nursing homes.

Just as the typical seminary campus today retains little of the older common trademarks, so too church congregations are not what they used to be. Blended families, divorced and single persons, as well as gays and lesbians, are also part of the changing scene in our churches today. Working parents must not only find ways to raise their children but, increasingly, ways to take care of grandparents.

In this rapidly changing demographic situation, we need to listen to the Creator's probing question, "Where are you?" Like Adam and Eve, we are in transit and must pay attention to where we actually are, not where we would like to be. A first step toward a reordering of conventional patterns is to recognize that, while we are different as to age and background, everyone begins somewhere.

II

What we all begin with is our common humanity. We are created beings, which means that we are here not of our own choosing. And much of who and what we are comes to us with our creation, and without our choosing, such as our sexuality, our genetic and hereditary legacy, our left- or right-brain disposition, and our finite susceptibility to disease and inevitable death. Beyond these natural, common human bonds, we learn to communicate by voice or gesture, and we can experience joy and sorrow, pleasure and pain. We see and taste and hear and smell and touch, and we can respond to beauty and music because we all come endowed with a sense of awe and wonder.

The biblical and theological way of talking about our common humanity is to link our finitude with our creation in "the image of God" (Gen. 1:26f.). The *imago Dei*, interpreters have argued, must mean that something about us—our reason, soul, or conscience—in some way reflects as in a mirror the essential being of the

Creator. Theologians have wrestled for centuries over the question of whether God's original image in us has been destroyed by sin or merely obscured. The apostle Paul sees a connection between "the first Adam" and Jesus Christ as "the second Adam," in whom God's image is restored and in whom we experience "a new creation" (cf. 1 Cor. 15:45, 47; 2 Cor. 5:17). Traditional theology often used the *imago Dei* as a way of elevating human nature above the animal kingdom and nature itself. But in more recent times, we have come to see that this argument can also be used in subtle ways to justify human exploitation of both the animal kingdom and the world of nature.

However we understand the biblical account of human creation, everyone begins somewhere with something common to us all. Carl Jung speaks of the "collective unconscious" which unites all peoples everywhere through symbols, images, dreams, fantasies, and archetypes. "In addition to our immediate consciousness," he wrote in an essay titled "The Concept of the Collective Unconscious," "there exists a second psychic system of a collective, universal, and impersonal nature which is identical to all individuals."

Like what? we may ask. When Arthur Miller's play *Death of a Salesman* was translated into Chinese and scheduled for production in a Beijing theater, many wondered what indoctrinated Marxists would make of a stereotypical American capitalist salesman. The presentation was received with warm and ready acceptance, in spite of the conflicting ideologies. It was apparent to the audience that Willy Loman, the salesman, was pushing not a product but himself; the emotional conflicts within the inner family circle—father, mother, and two carefree and disdainful sons—obviously struck a common human chord of recognition and sympathy.

The same kind of common human response to joy and grief, wherever those emotions are manifested, is seen in the sigh of relief when a little child is rescued from a narrow well shaft, in bystanders' cheers as a person first thought to be crushed by the San Francisco earthquake is found alive, in the revulsion widely expressed against a group of "wilding" teenagers who beat and raped a jogger in Central Park, or in the joy in the faces of the liberated peoples of Eastern Europe.

We might think that these human commonalities are so obvious as to be taken for granted. But while that may be so, particularly for artists, musicians, and a few others, it is not at all apparent that the basic essentials of our *humanum*, our elemental human nature, figure in any significant way in religious studies or theological education. It is not commonplace for courses in the Bible or theology to pay much attention to the human ties that unite a diverse class of very different individuals, or, for that matter, for those courses to pay attention to the individuals as unique persons who make up the class.

Teaching at most levels, and especially at the graduate level, means paying serious attention not to students but to the academic rubrics of the discipline: content, methodology, scholarly research, and extensive bibliographies. The assumption here is that the faculty knows best what is good for the student—all students—regardless of where they come from or what they bring with them. Carl Rogers, whose works on psychology have had great influence among theologians and preachers, once said that he started his career "with the firm view that individuals must be manipulated for their own good." This assumption, he added, rested upon the simplistic conviction that "what is taught is what is learned."

III

From the perspective of modern theological scholarship, it can come as a surprise to realize that, in the gospels, Jesus never manipulates people for their own good. He meets them where they are and as they are. He seldom preaches at them or lays down doctrinal or ethical rules and regulations. The gospels report Jesus in casual conversation with all kinds of people, and his message is usually conveyed by way of parables, stories, analogies, and references to the commonalities of life. In only the first few chapters of Mark, the shortest Gospel, Jesus uses simple words such as anger, bed, birds, brother, bride, cloth, country, eating, garment, hand, heal, heart, house, hunger, kin, life, meat, mother, physician, root, seed, sick, sister, son, sun, thorn, town, walk, wine, and so on. Such a simple vocabulary hardly s⌐ able to carry the good news.

Jesus doesn't provide us with an explanation of the meaning of the parables or add footnotes to bolster his point. The sayings of Jesus are quite unlike most lectures that we hear. They are not laid out didactically like the traditional three-point sermon. To grasp the meaning of Jesus' teachings requires our participation, and who we are and what we bring with us will have much to do with how we understand what Jesus has to say to us. As with a painting or a musical composition, the artist and the musician don't tell us in advance what we should see or hear. If the picture or the music is to come alive for us, we must enter into the creative process and identify ourselves—who we are and what we are—with what is before us.

On several occasions in the Gospels, Jesus seems almost reluctant to teach or preach because he assumes that his hearers already have the rudiments of the simple gospel. The long discourse with Nicodemus about being born again with water and the Spirit is replete with doctrinal and sacramental overtones. Nicodemus has difficulty following the drift, but the text tells us that he was a leading Pharisee, and Jesus responds to his naïve questions by asking a question of his own: "So you are a teacher of Israel . . . and you do not recognize such things?" (John 3:10, PHILLIPS). Nicodemus clearly is confused, but Jesus tells him that he brings with him the rich legacy of Jewish history and faith, enough to begin a search for further truth.

In another complicated Johannine passage, where Jesus speaks of knowing the truth that makes us free, his hearers reply that they have always been free. But Jesus says, "If you were the children of Abraham, you would do what Abraham did" (John 8:39). And when the rich man urges that his family be warned about the perils of judgment, Jesus says, "If they do not hear Moses and the prophets, neither will they be convinced if some one should rise from the dead" (Luke 16:31). In these passages, Jesus seems to be saying that we have all the essentials to get started. It is as if he were saying, "You already have a common human legacy about the deepest realities of faith and life; why don't you bring them with you and build upon what you have?" The evangelist, of course, implies that to bring what we have in order to go farther would mean recognizing Jesus as the Christ. But that is at the end of the quest, not the beginning.

Whatever the evangelists had in mind, Jesus himself seems to take it for granted that the signs of divine power and presence ought to be as obvious as casual conversation about the weather (cf. Matt. 16:1–4). If a sick person is healed, isn't that a sign that God is at hand and at work among us? "Why do you question thus in your hearts?" (Mark 2:8).

IV

What would it mean for seminaries and congregations to take seriously some of the simple things we have mentioned? Certainly it would mean a person-directed rather than a program-oriented perspective. It would mean accepting all kinds of people where they are and for what they are rather than expecting everyone to be more or less the same. It would mean developing degree programs and parish activities from the point of view of the diverse group of individuals actually present rather than according to some predetermined curriculum or program that assumes one size fits all. It would mean building upon what we have called the commonalities of our human nature, the essentials that bind us all together, without overriding our individual peculiarities. And it would mean discerning the signs of the times for the divine presence in our midst, wherever there is healing, caring, and what the King James Version of the Bible calls loving-kindness or mercy.

Is there any reason to expect that such things might happen? Perhaps the best hope for tomorrow's theological education and for church congregations lies in the changing demographic statistics mentioned earlier. The diversity of the seminary campus population suggests that the older, traditional conventions of scholarship based upon academic uniformity will be confronted by women, second-career people, blacks and other minority groups, and international and third-world students. All these constituencies have vested, personal involvements in their education. They are unimpressed with academic generalities and scholarly abstractions. They are very much alive to themselves, to who they are and what they want to contribute in their own way and on their own terms.

The makeup of the typical mainline church congregation is as diverse as the seminary campus. Denominational affiliation is less important for many church members than it used to be. More important for those who switch membership or come back to church after a long absence is the personal warmth of the pastor and the people, their openness in accepting others as persons, and their active participation in a caring ministry. These are the traits often expressed by older members of a congregation, but, more significantly, they are characteristic of blended families, divorced and single persons, gays and lesbians, and many of those involved in or skirting around the edges of the current interest in spirituality and New Age disciplines. If only some of these possibilities transpire, caring such as this would be the best kind of evangelistic outreach to young people who otherwise will be left out altogether, if congregations simply become older and less alert to what is going on around them.

The simple gospel, as distinct from a closed system of theology, is always open to change and innovation. It respects the old but expects the new. So the Christian scriptures are called the *New* Testament and at baptism we receive a *new* name, we learn a *new* commandment, we sing a *new* song, and we look forward to a *new* heaven and a *new* earth.

It may be noted that the Catholic Church in America will have a special problem in the near future related to a drastic decline in priestly vocations. Under the sponsorship of Lilly Endowment, Inc., such studies as Dean Hoge's *Future of Catholic Leadership: Responses to the Priest Shortage* underscore two major Catholic obstacles, the vow of celibacy and the exclusion of women from ordination. Tables and statistics reflecting the current make-up of Protestant seminary enrollments can be found in many places, for example, the Spring 1988 issue of *Theological Education,* published by the American Association of Theological Schools, with an extensive report by Ellis L. Larsen and James M. Shopshire, "A Profile of Contemporary Seminarians." One of the chapters asks the question, "What Can the Churches Expect?"

THREE

Seeing and Hearing the Gospel

Consider a few random New Testament texts: "Lord, when did we see thee hungry and feed thee?" (Matt. 25:37); "We never saw anything like this!" (Mark 2:12); "For mine eyes have seen thy salvation" (Simeon in Luke 2:30); "[Peter, John, and James] saw his glory" (Luke 9:32); "And [Zacchaeus] sought to see who Jesus was" (Luke 19:3); "Come and see" (Phillip to Nathaniel in John 1:46); "Come, see a man who told me all that I ever did" (John 4:29); "Though I was blind, now I see" (John 9:25); "[Some Greeks] wish to see Jesus" (John 12:21); "Something like scales fell from [Paul's] eyes, and he regained his sight" (Acts 9:18); "Write what you see in a book" (to John in Rev. 1:11).

There are dozens, maybe hundreds, of references to seeing in the Bible. The eye is the bodily organ of physical vision, but biblical psychology easily transposes the physical into the spiritual. To see signs of the divine presence or to see Jesus implies much more than keeping both eyes open. These and other such passages suggest that the topic is not physical sight but discernment, perception, and awareness—in other words, a special kind of knowledge and cognition. When the blind receive their sight, when Paul regains his vision, and when all kinds of people, such as Samaritans and Greeks, want to see Jesus, there is something more going on than wanting a close-up look at a celebrity.

Now, consider a few more random texts: "This is my beloved Son . . . listen to him" (Matt. 17:5); "And his ears were opened" (Mark 7:35); "Blessed . . . are those who hear the word of God" (Luke 11:28); "He who has ears to hear, let him hear" (Luke 14:35); "All the people hung upon his words" (Luke 11:28); "The dead will hear the voice of the Son of God, and those who hear will live" (John 5:25); "So faith comes from what is heard" (Rom. 10:17).

There are as many biblical references to hear, listen, harken, and so on as there are to see, look, and behold. Hearing the gospel or listening to Jesus corresponds to seeing the signs of God's salvation in the person of Jesus. Seeing or hearing the gospel, or being blind and deaf to the good news, suggests much more than physical abilities or disabilities. When the disciples of John the Baptist inquired of Jesus whether or not he was the Messiah, they were told, "Go and tell John what you have *seen* and *heard*" (Luke 7:22, emphasis added). The two most important biblical organs of perception, the eye and the ear, are frequently related, as in this early apostolic testimony:

> We are writing to you about something which has always existed yet which we ourselves actually saw and heard. . . . It was *life* which appeared before us: we saw it, we are eyewitnesses of it. . . . We really saw and heard what we are now writing you about.
>
> (1 John 1:1–3, PHILLIPS)

I

We do not usually think of theology, Bible study, or sermon preparation as seeing or hearing. They are, for the most part, intellectual exercises that depend on and make use of written texts. To see the divine presence in Jesus or to hear what he has to say would, for many of us, mean studying books on Christology or reading the commentaries on, say, the Sermon on the Mount. Careful examination of the written word will lead us, we hope, to the living Word. And what we will be mostly doing in this kind of search and research is thinking rather than seeing or hearing.

To interpret the gospel or to expound the scriptures usually implies intellectual reflection about the structure and meaning of doctrine or of texts. Such reflection, in turn, suggests some sort of linear, sequential, discursive development such as the creed (from creation to eschatology), liturgical worship (from invoca-tion to benediction), the conventional three-point sermon, the seasons of the Christian year, and the Bible itself (from Genesis to Revelation).

This sequential pattern is so much a part of our verbal, literate culture that we simply take it for granted. The books, magazines, and newspapers we read, as well as the education we receive in school, college, seminary, and graduate school, all move in this printed-page, line-by-line, precept-by-precept fashion. The same is true, on a different level, with radio, television, answering machines, and recorded messages—they also follow audiovisual sight-and-sound "bites."

A built-in feature of this sequential pattern, though not always apparent or acknowledged, is the intellectual imperative to make a point, to demonstrate a proposition, to come to a conclusion, or to persuade someone about something. Creeds and theologies are not known for offering options. Biblical exegesis, involving Hebrew and Greek and the best commentaries, presumably clarifies and explains the text. Sermons usually move from step to step toward some sort of conclusion.

The apologists of the early church, those who defended the faith as Socrates defended himself in Plato's *Apology*, began an intellectual tradition that persists to this day. It is the often exciting and frequently controversial question-and-answer method of Augustine, Anselm, Aquinas, Calvin, Schleiermacher, Barth, Tillich, and many more, both ancient and modern. To show the reasonableness of the faith, or at least to demonstrate that Christian beliefs are not irrational—this is certainly one of the great and grand trademarks of the Western theological tradition.

II

What would it mean if we applied the old aphorism "seeing is believing" to the interpretation of the gospel? How do we *see* the good news? Why in the Gospels do we read about so many persons, from the nativity to the resurrection, who "would see Jesus"? And when they saw him, what did they see? We have no evidence that Jesus looked any different from anyone else in his time. François Mauriac once noted that Judas betrayed Jesus with a kiss simply because the soldiers otherwise wouldn't have known how to pick him out of the crowd.

We don't know how or why Simeon could see salvation in the

face of the Christ child, or what Zacchaeus saw at dinner with Jesus, or what the Greeks with their philosophical tradition were looking for, or whether they found it. Artists down the centuries have tried to show us what Jesus looked like, but since we haven't a clue, all such visual images must be at best tantalizing and at worst sentimental.

The late Roland H. Bainton of Yale University, a Quaker whose interest in contemporary woodcuts surprised many when they opened his classic biography of Luther, edited a handsome volume, *Behold the Christ: A Portrayal of Christ in Words and Pictures* (1974). The same year, Frederick Buechner, whose religious novels have had a steady circulation, edited a large, illustrated volume called *The Faces of Jesus* (1974). Margaret R. Miles of Harvard University has more recently written an instructive work, *Image as Insight: Visual Understanding in Western Christianity and Secular Culture* (1985).

The perennial and continuing fascination with picturing, visualizing, and seeing the Christ figure is perhaps related to the common human instinct to retain and keep alive the memory of family and friends. Once upon a time that meant paintings, sketches, portraits, and sculptures, but today the memory of a person is easily kept alive through photography, film, and videocassettes.

Two well-known illustrations of this fascination with the presence of the Christ figure come to mind. One is the legend about Veronica, who supposedly wiped the sweating, bloodied brow of Jesus with a veil (or handkerchief) as he trudged on the road to Golgotha. The true image of his face (vera = true and icon = image, hence the name Veronica) supposedly was imprinted on the cloth that, in many Renaissance paintings, she is shown holding up for all to see. The second example of searching for the true image of the Christ is the Shroud of Turin, the preserved pall that, some claim, covered the dead Christ. The outline of his face on the cloth has been studied and subjected to all sorts of modern chemical and textile tests, but authenticity seems unlikely.

There is, by the way, a curious footnote to the Veronica legend. It seems she met and married Zacchaeus, and the two of them took off for somewhere in France as early Christian missionaries. There isn't a shred of proof, but how marvelous to think of one who sought to see Jesus teaming up with one who carried with her a visual reproduction of his face!

But we must now insist that all artistic, legendary, and fanciful efforts to depict the Jesus of the Gospels or, for that matter, the risen Christ, are beside the point when we seek to understand that "seeing is believing." In the Gospels, to see Jesus is always something more spiritual and profound than looking at a face. Let two further illustrations hint at this deeper level of seeing.

We have already noted what Jesus says to the disciples of John the Baptist; namely, they should tell John what they've "seen and heard." But what did they see and hear? Jesus tells them that "the blind receive their sight, the lame walk, lepers are cleansed, and the deaf hear, the dead are raised up, the poor have good news preached to them" (Luke 7:22). On Easter morning when Mary Magdalene and "the other Mary" (Matt. 28:1) went to the tomb, they were greeted by an angel who said, "I know that you seek Jesus. . . . He is not here. . . . he is going before you to Galilee; *there you will see him*" (Matt. 28:5–7, emphasis added). Why Galilee? What is to be "seen" there? Well, to go to Galilee is to be in the presence of Jesus who preached the Sermon on the Mount, healed the sick, and restored sight to the blind—the very credentials he offered to the disciples of John the Baptist. "He is not here"—he cannot be grasped or contained in an icon or a nostalgic image. His redemptive presence is in the world of those who need healing, comfort, love, and hope.

John Masefield, the English poet laureate, wrote an imaginary drama called *The Trial of Jesus* that has an interesting exchange between two legendary persons. Longinus, the traditional name of the Roman centurion who had charge of the crucifixion and who is supposed to have said, "Truly this was the Son of God" (Matt. 27:54), returns to Pilate's court to make his report. There he is drawn aside by Procula, the traditional name of Pilate's wife, who asks, "Do you think he is dead?" Longinus replies, "No, Lady, I don't." "Then where is he?" she asks. "Let loose in the world, Lady," he answers.

III

If "seeing is believing," we must also add that "faith comes from hearing" (Rom. 10:17). Sight and sound, looking and listening, are closely correlated in the biblical way of communicating the word of God. We tend to think of the word as written, but before the writing was the oral tradition, stories passed along by word-of-mouth; in the case of the gospel, the visual presence of Jesus was one with what he said. Jesus *is* the word of God not so much because we can read about him but because he personified the divine in all sorts of visual ways and because what he said was what God has to say to us.

There are differences, of course, between seeing and hearing. To see something or someone is to respond, as an observer and a participant. To hear something or someone is to participate by receiving, listening, and paying attention. Seeing is a visual, perceiving, discerning experience; hearing requires the reception of invisible spoken words. "Seeing the text," such as the scriptures, means moving along a visiospatial line in sequential order, with the option of returning again and again to reexamine words and meanings. "Hearing the word" requires awareness of a spoken voice behind the written words, with pauses, silences, cadences, and mnemonic and formulaic refrains, essential elements in orality that are distinct from literacy.

Such distinctions between seeing and hearing, literacy and orality, have been examined in detail by Walter J. Ong, S.J., in two innovative studies, *The Presence of the Word: Some Prolegomena for Cultural and Religious History* (1981) and *Orality and Literacy: The Technologizing of the World* (1982). Werner H. Kelber has applied Ong's research to New Testament studies in his important but largely overlooked work, *The Oral and the Written Gospel: The Hermeneutics of Speaking and Writing in the Synoptic Tradition, Mark, Paul, and Q* (1983).

The implications for preaching the oral and aural background of the scriptures are provocative and of peculiar relevance today when the manuscript sermon seems somehow impersonal and remote. How, for example, can a preacher anticipate how a sermon will be heard? But there is another aspect of "hearing the word" that needs emphasis.

The Bible equates hearing the word with obeying the word. When Moses stands between the people of Israel and his mountain encounter with the Almighty, the "hear and obey" words are as clear as a bell:

'Hear, O Israel, the statutes and the ordinances which I speak in your
hearing this day, and you shall learn them and be careful to do them.'
... [And the people replied,] 'Go near, and hear all that the Lord God
will say; and speak to us all that the Lord our God will speak to you;
and we will *hear and do it.*'

(Deut. 5:1, 27, emphasis added)

We find the same connection between hearing and doing in
the Gospels. When Jesus was told that his mother and brothers
were waiting to see him, he replied, "My mother and my brothers
are those who hear the word of God and do it" (Luke 8:21). And
when a well-meaning woman thought to honor Jesus by praising
his mother, he said, "Blessed rather are those who hear the word
of God and keep it" (Luke 11:28). To his own disciples, Jesus
said, "Many prophets and kings desired to see what you see . . .
and to hear what you hear" (Luke 10:24). Peter and John tell
their sceptical audience, "You must judge; for we cannot but
speak of what we have seen and heard" (Acts 4:19). We can sum
up all this with Isaiah's dire warning, that Paul repeats: " 'Hear
and hear, but do not understand; see and see, but do not
perceive.' Make the heart of this people fat, and their ears heavy,
and shut their eyes; lest they see with their eyes, and hear with
their ears, and understand with their hearts, and turn and be
healed" (Isa. 6:9–10; cf. Acts 28:26–27).

IV

To discern the divine presence in our midst and to tune our
ears to what God has to say to us is not something we can count
on, as if squinting our eyes or unplugging our ears would do the
trick. Anyone can, of course, see and hear *something*. As with a
fine painting or a symphony concert, *something* can be enjoyed
on even a casual level. The same can be said for the scriptures,
especially many of the psalms as well as the parables of Jesus. But
the trouble is that we often do not see what is right before our
eyes or hear clearly what is being said. Jesus scolded those who
could discern the signs of good and bad weather but were not
aware of the divine presence in their midst (Luke 12:54–56).
Alluding to Isaiah, Jesus told his disciples that he spoke to the
people in parables "because seeing they do not see, and hearing

they do not hear, nor do they understand" (Matt. 13:13; cf. Isa. 6:9–10). When the blind recovered their sight and the deaf were made to hear, many were aware only that a miracle had taken place. They did not *see* the kingdom in and around them, and they did not *hear* the words of life as something to do, keep, or obey.

Two illustrations, one secular and the other sacred, may help us sense deeper meanings and cadences in what we see and hear. For many years, Al Hirschfeld has been the presiding artistic genius of the entertainment world. His marvelous caricatures of famous persons of film and stage have graced the pages of *The New York*

Times, and collections and exhibits of his drawings appear regularly.

Anyone can see and appreciate these drawings on a surface level. But there is a hidden agenda in Hirschfeld's sketches. He has a daughter named Nina, and for many years he has hidden the name "Nina" at least once in every drawing and sometimes four or five times or more. To know about "Nina" and to examine the pictures with this hidden puzzle adds a dimension that we would not otherwise know or see. The accompanying reproduction is of John Williams, conductor of the Boston Pops Orchestra; Carol Channing; and the late Sammy Davis, Jr. After the stylized signature "Hirschfeld," there is the number "3." This means that the name "Nina" appears three times in the drawing.

The second illustration, regarding hearing rather than seeing, relates to the background story of the vastly popular hymn "Amazing Grace," the first verse of which is well known:

> Amazing grace! (how sweet the sound!)
>   That saved a wretch like me;
> I once was lost, but now am found;
>   Was blind, but now I see.

The words come across with immediate meaning and with ready reception, but at a deeper level, if we know the story, there is much more behind these lines than we would otherwise know. The hymn's London-born author, John Newton (1725–1807), was the son of a sea captain and went to sea himself at eleven years of age. He later engaged in the African slave trade and became a sea captain during the most dreadful years of the white traffic in black humanity. During the long sea voyages, he taught himself Hebrew and Greek and studied the Bible. During a storm at sea, he became a Christian and later sought ordination in the Church of England. He eventually took a parish in Olney, where he became a popular preacher, and with the poet William Cowper, a member of his congregation, published a hymnal, *Olney Hymns,* that contained nearly three hundred contributions by Newton. The original title of "Amazing Grace," by the way, was "Faith's Review and Expectation." Newton had a direct influence on William Wilberforce (1759–1833) who led the movement in Great Britain to abolish slavery, years before

Lincoln's Emancipation Proclamation of 1863. Newton prepared his own epitaph:

> John Newton, once an infidel and libertine, a servant of slaves in Africa, was, by the rich mercy of our Lord and Saviour, Jesus Christ, preserved, restored, pardoned, and appointed to preach the faith he had long laboured to destroy.

We do not need to know this story in order to participate in singing "Amazing Grace" and in hearing the simple but profound message it carriers. But to be aware of at least some of this background is to hear at a deeper level, just as to know about "Nina" is to see what is not on the surface.

FOUR

Starting Over Again

Few of us travel along life's way without setbacks, detours, and the frequent need to stop in our tracks and start all over again. Pilgrimage epics, biographies, autobiographies, and television serials all suggest that the quest for self-identity and the meaning of life involve constant and recurring obstacles that require new directions and fresh courses of action. If such epics and stories can be taken as root-metaphors or basic patterns of everyone's life, then the graph of our journey takes on a stop-start zigzag pattern.

The Bible also participates in this paradigm. The Creation, that brought order out of chaos and in which God saw that everything that was made was good, is soon distorted. After fitful starts and lost directions, everything is swept away in the time of Noah by a flood so a new beginning can be made. Biblical history moves back and forth, up and down. Promises are thwarted by perils; the great personalities and leading figures often speak prophetic words and take decisive actions, but just as often they resist the divine call and need to learn anew what God is doing in the world.

In the Gospels and in the apostolic writings, "starting over again" runs like a refrain in which words beginning with the prefix "re," such as repentance, redemption, reconciliation, renewal, regeneration, and resurrection, are common. The same is true of the word "new" and its cognates, beginning with the New Testament and ending with "a new heaven and a new earth."

One definition of the simple gospel can be derived by reflecting on this distinctive vocabulary. The normative seasons of the Christian year—Christmas, Easter, and Pentecost—all celebrate the possibility of beginning over again. They are not just exercises in hope and optimism but emerge out of darkness and despair. Let us see how this is so.

I

The numerous images associated with the Advent–Christmas season, in both its secular and sacred traditions, attest to its widespread and enduring appeal. Christmas comes at the end of the year and looks forward to a new year's day. The winter solstice (December 21), when, as "solstice" implies, the sun "stands still," exemplifies the irony of Advent, when the sun's heat and light seem to fade and yet candles, yule log fires, and bright lights symbolically anticipate the sun's return. Ending and beginning tend to coalesce.

The same collusion appears in the hymnal, where the darkness of Advent precedes and anticipates the joyful, exuberant Christmas carols.

> O come, Thou Dayspring, come and cheer
>   Our Spirits by Thine advent here;
> Disperse the gloomy clouds of night,
>   And death's dark shadows put to flight.
> . . . .
> It came upon a midnight clear. . . .
>   The world in solemn stillness lay.

The same sequence of ending and beginning marks the transition from Good Friday to Easter. And the same images of darkness and light recur. At the time of the crucifixion, "There was darkness over the whole land . . . while the sun's light failed" (Luke 23:44, 45). The Easter resurrection occurs "on the first day of the week . . . while it was still dark" (John 20:1), and the dawn of a new day lights up an unexpected new beginning.

Once more, the paradigm is repeated in the transition from the Ascension, when the historical Jesus is removed from sight, to Pentecost, when the Holy Spirit descends on the perplexed followers of Jesus. The sadness and sorrow caused by the death of Christ, seen in the two disciples of Emmaus, becomes compounded by the departure of the risen Christ at the Ascension. But the Spirit makes present the absent Christ and

fulfills Jesus' word to the disciples that the Spi[ ]
into all the truth" (John 16:13).

The seasonal festivals of the Christian[ ]
movement from darkness to light, from or[ ]
beginning, from seeming despair to the promise of tomo[ ]
also find parallel expression in Christian faith and experience.
Perhaps John of the Cross and his image of the "dark night of the
soul" can stand not only for the Christian mystical tradition but
also for every person's pilgrimage from the "slough of despond"
to the "celestial city." Mystics and contemplatives in every age
tell us repeatedly that the Christian ever and again must "stop,
look, and listen," as the old railroad crossing sign once warned
us, if we are to move forward out of darkness into light. Let some
personal lines adapted from a Christmas card originally prepared
by my father for his congregation illustrate the point:

> When Christ the Lord was born,
> It was starlight,
> Not sunlight.
>
> When the Christmas angels sang
> The Gloria in Excelsis,
> It was midnight.
>
> When on Calvary, the Savior of the world
> Opened the Kingdom of Heaven to all believers,
> There was darkness over the whole land.
>
> My soul: Why is this? Why does God
> Come in the shadows? Is it because
> The whole world is still, and our eyes are clear?
>
> Listen then! A sound from heaven
> As of a rushing mighty wind
> With cloven tongues of fire!
>
> "Behold, I make all things new."

II

What we have been talking about, stopping and starting over
again, is also one way of describing the history of theology and of
the church. Conventional wisdom about theology and the church

The Simple Gospel

_..._plies a certain rigidity and unchanging allegiance to standards and norms established years ago. But even a cursory survey reveals that every new era and every new exposition of the faith claims to close the previous period because the old era has ended, requiring a new venture for a new age.

We must observe, of course, that not all new beginnings were destined to endure or prove creative. False starts were made, and visions of a new tomorrow often went unfulfilled. After the powerful presence of Augustine, the period of the so-called Dark Ages must have been a dismal time to be alive and with little expectation of the Renaissance or the Reformation yet to come. Barbara W. Tuchman's marvelous historical survey, _A Distant Mirror: The Calamitous Fourteenth Century,_ Umberto Eco's novel, _The Name of the Rose,_ and the apocalyptic paintings of Hieronymus Bosch all suggest a great stretch of time when theology and the church seemed to stand still. Even after the Reformation, which was hailed as a radical new beginning, Protestants indulged in uncreative intramural disputes that failed to advance the cause of Christian truth.

But whatever may be said of the past, more modern efforts at theological reconstruction almost invariably hint at attempting something new and recreative. For example, the first volume of Karl Barth's massive _Church Dogmatics_ (1932) was actually a rewrite of an earlier book called _Christian Dogmatics_ (1927). The change from "Christian" to "Church" was, for Barth, intentional and theologically significant and, at the time of writing, both innovative and controversial. "Dogmatics," he wrote in _Church Dogmatics,_ is not "a 'free' science, but one bound to the sphere of the church where, and where alone, it is possible and sensible. . . . I have cut out in this second issue of the book everything that in the first issue might give the slightest appearance of giving to theology a basis, support, or even a mere justification in the way of existential philosophy" (p. ix). In other words, Barth stopped in order to start over again.

Georgia Harkness (1891-1974), practically the only woman teaching theology in her generation, wrote a widely used textbook entitled _Understanding the Christian Faith_ (1947). There was a great flurry of books about this time trying to demonstrate the reasonableness of Christian truth, with titles such as *Beliefs That Matter, A Faith for Today, The Reason for Living, The Logic of Belief, The Meaning and Truth of Religion.* In her introduction, Harkness wrote, "Everywhere are persons . . . who would seriously like to know what a Christian may believe. . . . This book is . . . for the open-minded seeker" (pp. 13–14).

Paul Tillich indicated his reason for producing a three-volume *Systematic Theology* by writing, "My purpose . . . has been to present the method and structure of a theological system written from an apologetic point of view and carried through in a continuous correlation with philosophy" (p. vii).

These three theologies of our recent past have almost nothing in common except that each one assumed it was starting over again, leaving behind older traditions and experimenting with new methods. Now let us look at three more contemporary examples.

John Macquarrie's *Principles of Christian Theology* (1966) has had a wide circulation as a textbook in both Great Britain and America. "The theological task," writes Macquarrie, "needs to be done over and over again, as new problems, new situations, and new knowledge come along" (p. vii). The "new" for Macquarrie relates to his appreciation of Martin Heidegger's philosophy and his praise for Karl Rahner's theology.

Geoffrey Wainwright's *Doxology: The Praise of God in Worship, Doctrine, and Life: A Systematic Theology* (1980), proposes a "doxological" approach to doctrinal theology. "In recent years," he writes in the preface, "there has indeed been a growing awareness of the links between worship and doctrine, but writers have still usually stopped short after a paragraph or two on the subject."

Peter C. Hodgson and Robert King are the coauthors of a popular text, *Christian Theology: An Introduction to Its Traditions and Tasks* (1982). "The purpose of this work," they state, "is twofold: (1) to introduce the student of theology to the Christian tradition by setting forth in brief compass its primary shape and substance, and (2) to pose the issues for systematic theology in the present day by showing how that tradition has been challenged and transformed under the pressures of modern thought" (p. vii).

III

If we were to extend this kind of survey to include representative examples of black, feminist, liberation, process, narrative, and postliberal theologies, the stop-and-go pattern would be even more apparent. What is involved in most of these current emphases is not so much a renewal of the doctrinal deposit of the past as a distancing from traditions that now seem inadequate in pursuit of a radically new perspective. The literature for each of the newer theological emphases has grown enormously in the past decade and is likely to continue to expand. Let us look at just three early examples of these radically innovative approaches.

In *God of the Oppressed* (1975), James H. Cone proposes a new way of looking at black theology. It is not, he insists, a variety of the Western theological tradition as taught in mostly white seminaries, but consciously and deliberately based upon the black experience as it emerged out of Africa and took expression in American slavery. "There can be no black theology which does not take the black experience as a source for its starting point. . . . For theology to be black, it must reflect upon what it means to be black" (p. 18). In Cone's subsequent writings, as with many other black theologians, a full stop was made some years ago that requires attention to new sociological studies. For the most part, black theology has not disengaged itself from the Bible or the person of Jesus Christ, but it insists that the biblical and christological tradition be interpreted from a black perspective.

The emancipation declaration for liberation theology is Gustavo Gutiérrez's pioneering work, *A Theology of Liberation* (first published in Spanish in 1971 with more than a dozen English translations of recent date). Much has been written about liberation theology since this early work, but the basic thesis of the movement persists. Gutiérrez puts it plainly: "The theology of liberation attempts to reflect on the experience and meaning of the faith based on a commitment to abolish injustice and to build a new society" (p. 307). The Latin America situation, out of which liberation theology emerged, represents a particular complexity, but the basic presuppositions of the movement, as many argue, pertain to other cultural and church traditions, perhaps especially in the so-called third world or two-thirds world.

Without any question, the most prolific and radical emphasis today is provided in the variety and creativity of feminist theology. It is quite impossible to keep up with the burgeoning feminist literature in all fields; given the growing numbers of women seminarians and teachers of religious subjects, it seems certain that this accent will become even more articulate. To select but one representative from this diverse movement must prove arbitrary, but Sallie McFague can perhaps serve as an example. All religious language, McFague maintains, is figurative, imagistic, and metaphorical. The parables of Jesus remind us that the Kingdom of God, which she calls a "root-metaphor," can be "likened to many things but not described directly or unambiguously." She suggests that "God as friend" is a possible genderless way of thinking, but even more important for a contemporary theology in our nuclear age is the necessity to experiment with new ways of expressing the Christian root-metaphors, always remembering that theological concepts must be partial and hypothetical. As to her own point of view, she writes in *Metaphorical Theology: Models of God in Religious Language* (1982) that "it comes out of a post-Enlightenment, Protestant, feminist perspective, a perspective which I would characterize as skeptical, relativistic, prophetic, and iconoclastic. It is more aware of the discontinuities between God and the world than of the continuities" (p. x). "In order to do theology," she writes in *Models of God: Theology for an Ecological, Nuclear Age,* (1987), "one must in each epoch do it differently" (p. 30).

In addition to these newer approaches to theology, there are some significant discussions not so much of theology itself but of ways and means to do theology. Edward Farley's *Theologia: The Fragmentation and Unity of Theological Education* (1983) has appealed to a wide audience, as has George A. Lindbeck's *The Nature of Doctrine: Religion and Theology in a Postliberal Age* (1984). Schubert M. Ogden's *On Theology* (1986) is typical of many articles and books that discuss theological methodology. Once again, the common denominator for such studies is the need to break away from past methods and procedures and launch out into the future with new proposals.

IV

Suppose now we revert to the previous discussion about the normative seasons of the Christian year: Advent–Christmas, Good Friday–Easter, Ascension–Pentecost. In these annual festivals, as we noted earlier, the new comes out of the old: the Christ child promises a new beginning in the midst of darkness at the nadir of the year; we can sing about "the wondrous cross" because "Jesus Christ is risen today"; and we can celebrate the presence of the living Christ because of the witness of the Holy Spirit.

But in every case, beginning over again entails risk and uncertainty. There is something untried and unknown about new prospects that can create a certain anxiety. There is surely something tenuous, as all parents know instinctively, about watching a child confront an uncertain future. We may call the funeral or memorial service "a witness to the resurrection," but grief is tenacious, and no one really knows what goes on after death. We may rejoice in the power of the Spirit, but the Spirit "bloweth where it listeth" (John 3:8, KJV); we have no control over it and cannot manipulate it for our own purposes.

This tentative aspect of the great seasons of the Christian year corresponds with the survey of recent theological trends we have just been discussing. The theologians advocating a new beginning are mostly aware of the risks they take and the possibility of obstacles and pitfalls on the path into even the immediate future. The possible dangers in stopping in one's tracks to start out anew is one reason ultraconservatives, both Catholic and Protestant, feel more secure with past, established traditions. Protestant evangelicalism, whatever else its merits, has not distinguished itself for innovative historical scholarship, for creative programs of social justice, or for the construction of theological systems and methodologies that could give new life to older traditions. Many Catholic theologians, especially in America, are eager to move forward, building on the promises of Vatican II, but find themselves threatened by the current restrictive mood in Rome and by such backward-looking scholasticism as in the newly proposed *Catechism for the Universal Church* (1990).

Those who accept the challenge and the risk of moving ahead and beyond will need not only courage and perseverance but sustaining faith and indomitable hope.

FIVE

Angels Unawares

What do the following familiar fairy tales and other stories have in common: "Snow White," "Little Red Riding Hood," "Cinderella," "Pinocchio," "Alice in Wonderland," and "The Wizard of Oz"? Well, many things, no doubt, such as their perennial appeal for both children and adults. But of special significance is the common thread of someone who appears at a crucial moment in the story to lend a helping hand or save a victim from evil witches or a fate worse than death. Serious volumes have been written interpreting children's stories mythologically and psychologically, but both young and old instinctively respond to a story of derring-do in which faith, hope, and love triumph over cunning, poison potions, and evil spells. And almost always a fairy godmother or the equivalent comes to the rescue in the nick of time.

In the chancel of Princeton University's neogothic chapel there is a series of four elongated stained-glass windows depicting Dante's *Divine Comedy,* Malory's *Death of Arthur* (or the Quest of the Holy Grail), Milton's *Paradise Lost,* and Bunyan's *Pilgrim's Progress.* These four classic narrative allegories of the search for the meaning of life, like children's fairy tales, all describe in elaborate detail life's ordeals and victories by including helpers, guides, and friends who appear from time to time along life's highway. Virgil leads Dante through the underworld, the Lady of the Lake and Galahad vindicate the death of Arthur, the archangel Michael defeats Satan and sets the stage for humanity's redemption in Christ, and the pilgrim Christian, with the help of his companions Faithful and Hopeful, eventually comes to the Celestial City.

I

From the perspective of the classic fairy tales and the great epic allegories, we may now explore the proposition that we often experience the divine presence in our midst when someone appears to intercede on our behalf. Frequently in the Bible and in later Christian history, this sort of divine intervention is associated with an angel of the Lord or with prayers to the saints. But whatever may be said for angels and saints, there may be a simple way to remythologize what otherwise would seem to many to be mysterious and ethereal. Can we not say simply that God often comes to us through others? Let three personal experiences illustrate the principle.

My earliest childhood memory is of being lost in Chicago near McCormick Theological Seminary. My father was a part-time lecturer in theology at the seminary and the minister of the nearby Fullerton Avenue Presbyterian Church. I remember stopping at a fire station and asking for a drink of water. The firefighters must have sensed that something was wrong, but I was not old enough to tell them my name or address. After some minutes, as I examined the red hook-and-ladder fire truck, a person whom I didn't know came along, took me by the hand, and led me back home. Sometime later, I learned that my guardian angel was Andrew C. Zenos, a professor of New Testament at McCormick and a good friend of my father. Maybe he knew that I was missing and simply went out to look for me. Years later, I discovered among some old books I was about to throw out a little volume called *The Teaching of Jesus*, written by Dr. Zenos, with this frontispiece inscription: *To Hugh Thomson Kerr, Jr., on the day of his baptism . . . with love from the author*. I suppose I remember the early episode because being lost is always a traumatic experience, and in my case the incident seemed, on later reflection, to parallel the Parable of the Prodigal Son. But as the lost and found episode has stuck in my mind all these years, I also recall feeling regret that I never took occasion to thank my benefactor.

In my sophomore year in college, studies and thinking about my future weren't really absorbing my attention. In a halfhearted way, I was planning to major in philosophy, but I had failed a course in geology which I should never have taken, and so I put in two months of summer school to make up the failure and to test a general survey course on philosophy. But, as I recall, my heart wasn't in my studies until a curious twist changed things completely.

One day in the summer philosophy class, a friend of mine went to see the instructor about something in his midterm paper. The professor tried to explain, but my friend said that he really wasn't much interested in philosophy, at least not as much as his friend Kerr who was planning to major in the department. The next day, the teacher asked me to stay after class, and of course I was terrified.

Dr. Norton was uncommonly kind and attentive, encouraging me beyond my wildest dreams, suggesting that my paper indicated a special interest in ethical theory. It was the first time in my life that a teacher had taken a personal interest in me. I went on to receive honors in philosophy and was awarded a senior prize in ethics. The rest of my courses fell into place. I learned how to write an exam, and studies and books became exciting and congenial. In this example, there were two intercessors, a classmate and a teacher, who took time to talk to a shy and diffident sophomore. I remind my classmate of my indebtedness whenever I see him, but I regret that I never had a chance to thank the professor.

There is a curious parallel to this story. When Jimmy Stewart, the film star, was being honored on Princeton University's 1990 Alumni Day as a member of the class of 1932 (the year after my class, 1931), he told an audience of alumni, alumnae, and students that he owed his success to a summer makeup class!

A third personal experience when someone made a decisive difference in my life came in mid-career. As a teacher of theology, my inclination was toward a structured and reasoned explication of Christian doctrine. But this approach was becoming increasingly unsatisfying without my knowing why, and a friendly family physician urged me to seek counsel from a therapist whom he trusted. Without much enthusiasm or expectation, I made an appointment with Dr. Ursula Knoll, who had studied at the Jung Institute in Zurich. This was not a typical in-depth, psychoanalytic approach but more a series of conversations that went on once or twice a week for about two years.

My first assignment was to read Jung's big book, *Psychology and Alchemy,* on two topics that were as remote from where I was at the moment as could be imagined. But after I got into the discussion, I was hooked. I learned a whole new language about symbols, archetypes, and the collective unconscious. It was a new world, and I felt like Dorothy when she entered the multihued sphere of Oz and said to her dog, Toto, "This isn't Kansas any more."

This mid-career experience changed the direction and quality of my life, both personally and professionally. Theology was never the same again. While I didn't receive any direct vision of the divine or experience anything like a mystical union with the Absolute, my life's pilgrimage changed directions and a new sense of meaning and purpose took hold of me. Once again, I'm sorry that I never told Dr. Knoll what all this meant to me.

II

These personal reminiscences are recounted for three reasons. First, everyone probably has had similar experiences. We may forget them or not bring them forward into consciousness partly because we like to think we are self-sufficient and partly because gratitude to others is something of a lost art these days. I have noted my own remorse at not thanking my benefactors. Most of us, I would venture, are in the same boat. I once asked students in a theology class if someone had done something special for them recently and whether they had responded with a note of thanks. Several students came up to me after class and said they were going to their rooms to write a long-overdue letter. Of the ten lepers whom Jesus healed, only one, a Samaritan, glorified God (cf. Luke 17:11–19).

In the second place, I don't pretend to know whether the people who interceded on my behalf were divine emissaries or not. I am inclined to think they were. I've come to feel strongly that God becomes real and present to us through other people, and I think it happens all the time without our knowing or paying attention. This, in its simplest essence, is what incarnation means.

In the third place, it is important to distinguish this awareness of the divine presence from "foxhole religion," Bonhoeffer's

"God of the gaps," the "hail Mary" football pass, or the ancient notion of deus ex machina. We are not talking about special privileges but about experiences that are commonplace and part of our day-to-day humanity. Reinhold Niebuhr, in his well-known sermon, "The Providence of God" (in *Discerning the Signs of the Times*), warned against interpreting God's providence as if the pious could lobby in the courts of the Almighty for their private benefit when it is the same God who "sends rain on the just and on the unjust" (Matt. 5:45). We're not talking about what we can do to win divine favor but what God can do without our knowing how or why. Often as not this happens when we least expect it, and the presence of God in our lives, after all, is not something that we can arrange for our own convenience.

Perhaps there is a correlation between our congenital ingratitude toward those who intercede for us and our blindness at not seeing God at work among us and within us. If we believe in a loving God, in a living Christ, and in a Spirit who moves at will, we can surely also believe that things will happen to us and for us if only we open our eyes and are receptive.

> I ask no dream, no prophet ecstasies,
>   No sudden rending of the veil of clay,
> No angel visitant, no opening skies;
>   But take the dimness of my soul away.

III

There is another level in this matter of discerning the divine presence that needs attention. As noted in the few personal experiences mentioned, intercession of what, on reflection, seems a God-send often results in a radical change of outlook.

The intervention of a fairy godmother in children's stories and the guides and helpers along the way in the epic allegories provide the resolution of a dilemma that otherwise seems intractable. In the process, a new sense of self emerges and, without being overly romantic about it, everyone "lives happily ever after." In theological terms, when God comes to us through others, we are not only shown the way out of an impasse, we get a new look at ourselves, and life takes on new meaning.

Those who have recorded their conversion experiences, such as Augustine, John Newton, Sojourner Truth, Leo Tolstoy, Ethel

Waters, Malcolm Muggeridge, and dozens of others, all testify to the awareness of a new self and a new life direction. But the best way to see how this works is to look at some instances in the Gospels where those who came into direct contact with Jesus found a new perception of themselves. After all, Jesus is the divine presence in person, the primal "God-send"; as someone has said, "Jesus brought God down to earth."

The encounter of the Samaritan woman with Jesus at Jacob's well (John 4:4–42) is a richly complicated passage with delicate and controversial discussions about worship, marriage, and the water of life. Jesus was not judgmental and did not moralize, but apparently the woman was deeply impressed by the exchange. In her excitement, she left her water pot by the well, fled back to her village, and blurted out to all who could hear, "Come, see a man who told me all that I ever did" (John 4:29). We don't know what happened to this woman or whether she knew who Jesus was, but her actions and the tone of her remark suggest that she found a new self-awareness.

This story, by the way, is one of several instances in the Gospels where Jesus is reported to have paid special and unconventional attention to women, in this case a Samaritan woman. When the disciples rejoined Jesus, "they marveled that he was talking with a woman" (John 4:27).

The first disciple called by Jesus was Levi (or Matthew), a tax collector (Matt. 9:9–13; Mark 2:13–17; Luke 5:27–32). The new recruit was apparently so astonished at Jesus' invitation that he decided to throw a big party for his friends to rejoice with him. Here we have, like the Samaritan woman, an ostracized outsider who becomes the recipient of Jesus' special favor. Legend holds that this first disciple was also the author of the first Gospel, though most scholars regard such authorship as unlikely. Anyway, whatever happened to this person later on, he must have felt something in the dynamic presence of Jesus that gave him joy and changed his life.

A little person with a little curiosity about Jesus, Zacchaeus perched himself in a sycamore tree along the route where Jesus and the crowd were to pass. "A chief tax collector, and rich" (Luke 19:2), he probably thought no one would notice him (cf. Luke 19:1–10). But Jesus spied him and invited himself to dinner. Zacchaeus, we read, "made haste and came down" (Luke

19:6). Someone once said that perhaps he was so astonished he fell out of the tree. Anyway, Jesus brought him down to earth, and it must have been an exhilarating and restorative experience for Zacchaeus, who may have been up a tree in more ways than one.

The Samaritan woman just wanted to talk with Jesus, Zacchaeus just wanted to see him, the woman with uncontrollable bleeding just wanted to touch the hem of his garment (cf. Mark 5:25–34; Luke 8:43–48), Mary just wanted to soothe his feet with ointment, and the common people heard him "gladly" (Mark 12:37). Whether these and others who came into contact with Jesus became disciples or believers, they apparently experienced the divine presence in their midst and found, in the process, a new sense of self-worth.

IV

It may appear that we oversimplify things when we put the emphasis upon new self-awareness. Surely the evangelists who record the instances of Jesus in contact with various kinds of people are not primarily interested in the psychology of self-esteem. Their concern is to present Jesus as the Savior who speaks words of eternal life, works miracles of healing, and proclaims the kingdom of God. It may be that those who write about their conversions found a new self-assurance, but their accounts can also be read as theological illustrations of the process from sin to salvation through the person of Christ. But whatever it means to be "saved," whether in the Gospels or in the lives of Christians in all ages, contact with Jesus, God's presence with us on earth, is like being born again into "a new creation" (2 Cor. 5:17).

We began by talking about experiences that most of us have when, unexpectedly, someone appears to lead us out of a blind alley and point us in a new direction. If Jesus is the prime example of this kind of intercession, is there, we may wonder, any correlation between his divine mission and the innumerable assists given us every day of our lives in more modest and simply human ways? Is the vast company of public servants, nurses, protectors of the environment, advocates of social justice, volunteers working for the homeless, middle-aged parents caring for their elderly parents, dedicated but frustrated teachers in inner-city schools, and on and on—are these individuals entitled to be called guardian angels? Are they in some way stand-ins or surrogates for the divine presence of God in Christ? Is this one way to define the simple gospel—as the good news that God comes into our lives in unexpected and everyday ways?

If that is possible, and if God's grace comes to us in simple as well as sacred ways through others, then we must also be reminded that "to whom much is given . . . will much be required" (Luke 12:48). The grace of God calls forth our gratitude to respond to intercessions on our behalf by interceding for others. The writer of the Epistle to the Hebrews makes this plain:

> Do not neglect to show hospitality to strangers, for thereby some have entertained angels unawares. Remember those who are in prison, as though in prison with them; and those who are ill-treated. . . . Let marriage be held in honor. . . . Keep your life free from love of money, and be content with what you have.
>
> (Heb. 13:2–5)

What I Owe to Christ, C. F. Andrews's immensely popular autobiography, tells how Andrews responded to the gift of God's presence in his life. An Anglican priest long disturbed by the plight of the poor and oppressed, he decided to go to India, where he became a close friend of Mahatma Gandhi. Played by Ian Charleson in the film *Gandhi* (1982), C. F. Andrews came alive for all who saw his behind-the-scenes, quiet Christian witness. Earlier, as a newly ordained priest, he tells in his autobiography how uncomfortable he became with the imprecatory psalms, the damnatory clauses of the Athanasian Creed, and the sterile orthodoxy of the Anglican Thirty-nine Articles. Going to India to work with Gandhi was C. F. Andrews's way of trying "to get back to the simplicity of the gospel."

SIX

My Kind of Theology

In the theology class of about forty seminarians mentioned earlier, I give each year a simple test to determine left- or right-brain dominance. It isn't very scientific, but the results often surprise the students. Only one or two come out strongly on the far left or the far right of the scale, with the big majority somewhere in the middle. In the way they process the data of reality and experience, left brain–dominant people (I'm one of them) tend to be sequential, logical, linear, verbal, and articulate; right brain–dominant people are intuitive, imagistic, pictorial, analogical, and connective. The difference has nothing to do with intelligence; a left brain–dominant person can learn to utilize the other side with a little effort (as I can testify), and the right brain–dominant person can learn to use the left side, especially as needed to write term papers and prepare for exams.

Thinking that members of the faculty might come out strongly on the left side, I gave the same test to an equal number of professors. I figured that many students come to seminary or divinity school for personal and emotional motives, perhaps hoping to build on and extend a commitment to Jesus Christ made recently or a few years ago. Teachers, so I imagined, because of the nature of their disciplines and the conventions of classroom lectures, would be highly rational and logical. But the professors scored almost exactly the same as the students. So, I concluded, rightly or wrongly, that the left hemisphere dominates the curriculum, with the considerable assistance of the library, the academic schedule, course requirements, and grades.

Almost everything about theological education, with the exception of worship, is left brain–oriented. Students with left-brain dominance have little trouble with classes, library research, or final exams, but pity the right-brained seminarians who find little in their education that seems congenial or compatible. How left- and right-brain dominance correlates with vocational decisions could be tested. Do left-brained students tend to go into graduate studies and end up as teachers, while right-brained seminarians head for the pastoral ministry and other forms of person-directed service?

I

There are, of course, many tests and instruments to suggest various personality traits. Everyone knows the difference between an introvert and an extrovert, a day person and a night person, a dualist (everything is either right or wrong, true or false) and multiplist (open to options). But what is the significance, if any, of such profiles? Three implications come to mind.

First, who and what we are will have much to do with how we read and study the Bible and books on theology. We will interpret the history of doctrine and of the church as we see things through the lens of our own persons. We will teach and preach and otherwise carry on our ministry in accord with who we are, whether we take time to find out our special characteristics or not. Inevitably, we will see things not as they are but as *we* are.

In the second place, who and what we are will determine not only how we read theology but how we formulate our own theology. Students and seminarians are constantly required, when making applications for admission, scholarship aid, ordination, or church positions, to prepare a personal autobiographical inventory and a brief statement of faith. Some of us have little difficulty with these assignments because we are used to thinking sequentially, but those who think intuitively cannot always cope with simple definitions or point-by-point structures. Whatever our personality tilt, our theology, our sermons, and our pastoral care will surely reflect the kind of person we happen to be.

The third reason why the person of the theologian, the preacher, or the pastor makes a difference concerns personal, social, and communal relationships. We might imagine that all of those of the same personality type would flock together, but that isn't necessarily so. In fact, opposites, as we all know, tend to attract each other, whether as roomates, friends, spouses, or partners. It would seem that we often find in others a compensating part of our own selves, and we easily make friends with those who fulfill in us something we lack. In any case, for teachers, preachers, and pastors, it is of crucial importance to heed the ancient prescription to know ourselves—and, we may add, to know others who are very different from us. This is of obvious significance in the area of pastoral care, where the diversity of personalities must be recognized regardless of who we are and how we see things.

II

While not putting too much weight on bicameral brain research, we might note that the history of theology tends to zigzag from one side to the other. We usually think of theology as an intellectual enterprise involving sequential structures and logical demonstrations. This is the way the subject has been taught in our seminaries and divinity schools, and this is the assumed methodology in courses on religious studies in colleges and universities. Though not as common as in previous times, preaching is also usually structured upon the linear development of a theme or exposition of a text.

But the history of theology shows us that for every systematic structure there is a corresponding mystical or contemplative emphasis, as if the intuitive and analogical side of human reflection were counterbalancing and correcting the rational, verbal aspect. The Bible itself provides evidence of this duality in the historical books and the psalms, in the Synoptics and John, and in the Pauline corpus and the Apocalypse.

In theology, the cathedral-like system of Thomas Aquinas needs the very different accent of Francis of Assisi. The medieval scholastics Duns Scotus and William Ockham were near contemporaries of such mystics as Catherine of Siena and Thomas à Kempis. The reformers Martin Luther and John Calvin were experts at debates and disquisitions at the same time that Teresa of Avila and John of the Cross were exploring pathways of the inner life. While Karl Barth and Paul Tillich were writing multiple volumes on systematic theology, Dietrich

Bonhoeffer and Evelyn Underhill were agonizing over the difficulty of being Christian in the modern world. Karl Rahner pushed his "theological investigations" to their theological and philosophical limits at the same time that Thomas Merton, taking a vow of silence, preached through his writings from a mystical pulpit in a Trappist monastery and, though a Westerner, began to peer wistfully at the mysterious East.

These correlations are no more precise than the interconnections of left- and right-brain hemispheres, but the emphases are distinct and apparently need each other for balance, correction, and mutual edification. And it must be noted that the distinctions are not exclusively absolutistic or predetermined and inexorable. Both Luther and Calvin, for example, wrote hymns. Barth was a lover of the music of Mozart, and Tillich was fascinated with modern art. On the other side of the equation, the contemplative tradition has never repudiated the doctrinal legacy of the theologians, and mystics would definitely insist that their writings and recorded experiences were as theological as those of the system makers.

III

Suppose now we ask how to go about constructing a theology of our own. "Constructing" is perhaps too loaded a word, since many would be uneasy with anything so organized. Suppose, then, we ask how any of us who have some special responsibility for teaching, preaching, or pastoral care would go about articulating and expressing the main points of Christian faith. If we were to pick and choose among the historical-theological examples available, who and what would attract us most, and why? Unless we just adopt unquestioningly someone else's theology, the matter of selecting from the past, filtering through our own persons, and projecting into today and tomorrow is not so easy.

We have been hinting that the person of the theologian or the person of the preacher has something to do with the kind of theology or sermon that emerges. Contemporary interest in autobiography, associated with psychohistory and the fascination with intimate television talk shows and interviews, takes for granted that the person of the person is an essential ingredient in understanding how we live and think and express ourselves.

Frederick Buechner, the novelist, preacher, and theologian, in the first installment of his own life story, writes, "My assumption is that the story of any one of us is in some measure the story of us all." If true, that would mean that we see and find ourselves in the lives of others and that our own biographies become involved in what we do and say. That assumption would also mean that the way we interpret the Christian faith would carry something of a personal signature.

This personal trademark is more conspicuous today than in previous times. Theology seems less and less a sequence of propositions and more and more a personal statement, a conviction rooted in a special context, or a social protest in the name of the God who has decreed a preferential option for the poor and oppressed. Black theology, for example, seems not so much a definable system as an expression of personal and racial hurt. Liberation theology manifests itself more as a critical and social perspective than as a doctrinal reformulation. Feminist theology has developed as a reproach to conventional patriarchal pretensions. If these and other contemporary emphases seem short on doctrinal definition, the anguish and eloquence of the person(s) behind the theology cannot be discounted.

To make this rather general discussion more personal, I would have to say for myself that my kind of theology, for what it's worth, has emerged out of a rather conventional, systematic sequence of doctrines to take on two characteristics I would not have foreseen some years ago. The first is a shift from a mostly Christocentric perspective to a more Spirit-centered view, and the second is a redistribution of theological luggage in the interests of traveling light.

Structures and systems are very important for me. I can see a correspondence between trying to get everything all together in theology and the contemporary concern to understand the environment as an implicative and interdependent system of the primal elements—earth, air, fire, and water. But I also reflect that if Christian faith can be structured and diagrammed, with the Christ figure at the center, as with the second article of the Apostles' Creed, it is important not to forget that the second article is followed by the third article on the Holy Spirit. To take this sequence seriously, I have come to believe, means restructuring and reimaging much of Christian faith.

IV

The cumulative direction of the Creed, as of much else in the classic doctrinal and liturgical tradition, positions the Holy Spirit as the fulfillment of God's redemptive purpose in Christ. The tendency with much Christian theology, ancient and modern, is to emphasize Christ with only a passing nod in the direction of the Spirit.

I have myself long held as a normative statement of this sequence what Calvin writes in the Book 3 of the *Institutes*. After discoursing at great length about the knowledge of God, creation, revelation, human sin, and the redemption accomplished by Christ, Book 3 begins with this connective clue: "The Holy Spirit is the bond by which Christ effectively unites us to himself." From one point of view, this would seem to cancel out everything that has gone before, but from another point of view, the Spirit sequence fulfills and makes meaningful all that has gone before in God's comprehensive plan of salvation.

We are not talking about the heresy associated with Joachim of Fiore (1135–1202), who interpreted the three articles of the Creed as successive epochs of revelation. In this scheme, the second article supersedes the first article, and the third article, concerning the Holy Spirit, supersedes both the first and the second articles. We are talking about the place of the Spirit in the process of redemption and within the classical trinitarian formulation, that Calvin accepted, that the three persons of the Trinity are coequal in divinity but separate and distinct regarding revelation and redemption. In addition to the library of volumes on the Trinity, there were numerous visual symbols that illustrate the relationships between the three persons. The isosceles triangle, the trefoil, and the triquetra are all designs frequently used as emblems of the interrelationships of the three persons of the Trinity:

Why is it important to give equal time and attention to the Holy Spirit? The reason is simple but has far-reaching theological significance. The historical Jesus; the Jesus of the Gospels; the spinner of parables and stories; the miracle worker; the prophet of the kingdom of God; the friend of the poor, the outcast, women and little children; the suffering, crucified servant—this historical Jesus is no longer present but absent. The New Testament is unambiguous about this. In addition to the ascension references ("he parted from them," Luke 24:51; "a cloud took him out of their sight," Acts 1:9), there are other allusions to the absence of the historical Jesus. The angels tell the women at the tomb, "He is not here" (Matt 28:6), and at Emmaus, after breaking bread with the two disciples, "he vanished out of their sight" (Luke 24:31). In John's Gospel, Jesus tells his disciples that he must "go away" (John 14:28) and that they will see him "no more" (John 16:16).

As we have noted elsewhere, the work of the Spirit, as Jesus promises his disciples, is to "teach you all things, and bring to your remembrance all that I have said. . . . [and] guide you into all truth" (John 14:26;16:12). This is the classic Christian sequence celebrated in creed, liturgy, and sacrament. The theology underlying this sequence suggests that the absent historical Jesus is made present as the risen Lord by the Spirit. This is the same Spirit that brooded over the preformal waters of creation, that acted as the agent of conception for the birth of Jesus, that descended upon the bewildered crowd at Pentecost, and that moves among us freely, without our control or manipulation, like the wind.

Without further elaboration, we can think of three implications of a Spirit-centered theology. For one thing, the Spirit is nameless and, for that reason, provides a breakthrough in our current gender dilemma over the names for deity. In the second place, emphasis on the Spirit could lift our often fuzzy and sentimental "Jesus-ology" to a higher level, where the cosmic Christ "sits at the right hand of God" but is made present in our midst and within us by the Spirit. And in the third place, discussions between Christians and Jews, and with persons practicing other religions as well as new forms of spirituality, might get beyond the usual temptation toward Christian triumphalism, in which traditional Christology frustrates sincere efforts at mutual understanding.

V

In addition to sensing a new Spirit accent in my kind of theology, and after teaching theology for fifty years, I find that things get briefer and simpler. I still feel comfortable with the big systems, and I can appreciate the theologians' urge to get everything together without any dangling threads. Like the medieval cathedral, a comprehensive system acts as a biblical dictionary and an encyclopedia of church history. But the urge toward completeness can easily become a reason for thinking that bigger is better and longer is more persuasive. Definitions of the simple gospel may leave out something essential, but the long form may try to say too much.

The Bible itself presents us with both a long and a short form, depending on how we use it. Apart from the biblical scholars, few of us ever hope to master the Bible as a whole, and so we settle for our own shorter and more manageable canons. And extensive as it is, the Bible recognizes certain necessary limitations. Three examples from the New Testament suggest that not everything can be included. John's Gospel, the longest of the four, concludes, "But there are also many other things which Jesus did; were every one of them to be written, I suppose that the world itself could not contain the books that would be written" (John 21:25). The apostle Paul despairs of saying all that could be said about the grace of Jesus Christ, the "inexpressible gift," and falls back on doxology—"Thanks be to God!" (2 Cor. 9:15). The writer of the Epistle to the Hebrews, recounting the long list of the faithful, gives up calling the roll and says, "What more shall I say? For time would fail me" (Heb. 11:32). Even as big as it is, the Bible might have been bigger, but such references as these hint that the limitations of space, language, and time require us to settle for less.

The Lord's Prayer, for example, says nothing about thanksgiving, but it says enough. The Creed omits mention of scripture, the life and teachings of Jesus, and the sacraments, but for liturgical purposes it is quite sufficient. "A Brief Statement of Faith" for the Presbyterian Church (U.S.A.) is made up of eighty short statements, beginning with "In life and death we belong to God" and ending with the Gloria. It is meant for worship services and doesn't pretend to say everything but to say what is needed for the moment.

Whatever reasons there may be for a short form of the faith (e.g., religious education of children and youth), we must remember that any definition of the simple gospel is dependent upon and related to the whole corpus of scripture and the whole theological tradition. My kind of theology at long last may be content with two or three essentials, and it is a vast relief to let go a lot of luggage that once seemed so necessary. But I've come to where I am in the faith by way of a long and winding pilgrimage of search and struggle. I'm not yet in sight of the Celestial City because I'm still on the road.

The simple gospel, as we noted at the beginning, is profound, not simplistic. But to repeat an aphorism of C. S. Lewis's, if we can't put the Christian faith into words that anyone can grasp, it probably means that we either don't understand it, or we don't believe it.

SEVEN

The Flame, Not the Ashes

There is an ancient proverb that admonishes, "From the fires of the past, carry the flame, not the ashes." Flame and fire have always been associated with purification rites, the possibility of renewal, and immortality and eternal life. Mircea Eliade's fascinating but not widely known book, *The Forge and the Crucible: The Origins and Structures of Alchemy* (1962), details fire rituals among primitive peoples and pays special attention to medieval alchemy. In the process of combining metals and other substances, new beginnings were anticipated that would leave behind the dross, the ashes, and the dregs. Jung observed the same kind of fiery amalgams in many patients' dreams and fantasies, even though they knew nothing of alchemy or the complicated mythology of the forge and the crucible.

I

The purifying and renewing power of the flame is everywhere attested, from the Promethean myth of snatching fire from Zeus' lightning bolts to the Mithric Zoroastrian rituals of lighting tapers and fires as recorded in the hymn to Ahura-Mazda:

> We worship the Spirit Divine
> . . . .
> The flame of our holy love.

(See the charming Christmas story, *The Other Wise Man*, by Henry van Dyke, first published in 1895 and still in print.)

It should be no surprise to find the flame and the fire often symbolizing important biblical instances of the divine presence. God's covenant with Abraham is marked by "a flaming torch" (Gen. 15:17); Moses encounters the Almighty "in a flame of fire out of the midst of a bush" (Ex. 3:2); the children of Israel are led out of Egypt "by day in a pillar of cloud . . . and by night in a pillar of fire" (Ex. 13:21); on Mount Sinai "the glory of the Lord was like a devouring fire" (Ex. 24:17; cf. Deut. 4:24); Elijah on Mount Carmel challenges the prophets of Baal with the God "who answers by fire" (1 Kings 18:24); and, after passing his prophet's mantle over to Elisha, we read that Elijah is translated into heaven by "a chariot of fire and horses of fire" (2 Kings 2:11).

These are only a few of the hundreds of references to fire and flame in the Hebrew scriptures. In the New Testament, fire often appears as a purifying agent, as in the ominous threat of being cast into the fire (e.g., Matt. 13:42), but the Pentecost experience of "tongues as of fire" (Acts 2:3) is surely a crucial reference to the work and presence of the Holy Spirit. In the Apocalypse, after "Death and Hades were thrown into the lake of fire," the Seer envisions "a new heaven and a new earth," and the one who spoke from the throne said, "Behold, I make all things new" (Rev. 20:14; 21:1, 5).

Carrying the flame but not the ashes has always characterized reform movements in Christian thought and in church history. Not everything in the scriptures is worth carrying forward; indeed, the canon of authorized writings, however ambiguous, is itself an attempt to separate the living word from extraneous material. The creeds and confessions of the church tend to discriminate between what is essential and what is only ephemeral or polemical. The Renaissance tried to recover the mood of the Greco-Roman culture, while the Reformation cut through the overload of medieval scholasticism in order to renew the spirit of the Judeo-Christian mythos. In more modern times, the Enlightenment spirit pervaded both biblical studies and doctrinal interpretation, resulting in the exciting, if often naïvely confident, liberal, rational pursuit of truth, whether religious or secular. No matter that today it is fashionable to decry the legacy of the Enlightenment and speak instead of postliberalism or postmodernism, the eighteenth and nineteenth centuries must have been times of great exhilaration.

Most biblical interpreters, preachers of sermons, and writers of religious articles and books imagine that they are refining a fresh insight, a new light—like the phoenix rising to new life from the ashes of its pyre—possibly a torch of flaming truth to be passed on to future generations.

The perfect example of renewing the past, of separating wheat from chaff, of forging a lamp to lead through the darkness is, of course, Jesus himself. In the Sermon on the Mount (Matt. 5–7), perhaps reminiscent of other mounts where the presence of the divine was revealed in flame and fire, Jesus repeatedly juxtaposes what was held to be true and sacred in the past with what, in his own person, is being disclosed for a new day and age. The Beatitudes seem a reversal of common sense. "You have heard that it was said . . . but I say to you . . . love your enemies . . . beware of practicing your piety . . . do not be anxious" (cf. Matt. 5:3–12).

There has always been a lively debate about interpreting Jesus' intent regarding the traditions of the past. Some think that everything points to radical reversal, but Jesus himself emphasizes that the law and the prophets are not to be abolished but fulfilled (Matt. 5:17). The vision on the Mount of Transfiguration has Jesus flanked by Moses and Elijah, and the law and the prophets are frequently cited by Jesus when he talks with those looking for new truth: Nicodemus (John 3:10; cf. John 8:39); the rich man and Lazarus (Luke 16:31); the rich young ruler (Matt. 19:17); the good Samaritan (Luke 10:25–37); and the overturning of the money changers in the temple (Mark 11:17). In all such instances, Jesus implies that his hearers ought to draw from their traditions, that they should already know where to find the answers to many of their problems, and that the Hebrew scriptures have not been annulled or superseded.

II

The dialectic between flame and ashes, new and old, yesterday and today has occupied alert minds in every age. Each new generation harbors the conceit that it can solve or transcend previous stalemates and prescribe paths toward renewal and rebirth. Theologically, this takes the form of "re-membering," not only in the sense of recalling the past but of putting it back together again for today.

The Reformation under Luther and Calvin was such a revivifying movement in early Protestantism, and Vatican

Council II under Pope John XXIII was a more recent but similar revival within modern Catholicism. In both instances, the new day dawning emerged out of the ashes of the past with the heady expectation that the fire and passion of the essential gospel would be rediscovered and carried like an Olympian torch into a new age. The basic issue here is the determination of the living tradition that ever and again must be handed over from accretions of history or convention that can and should be superseded.

Jaroslav Pelikan, in *The Vindication of Tradition*, says that "tradition is the living faith of the dead, traditionalism is the dead faith of the living" (p. 65). In the marvelous musical *Fiddler on the Roof*, based on a story by Sholem Aleichem, the Russian Jew Tevye begins with a plaintive song about tradition and asks, "What would we be without our tradition?"

It is not easy to distinguish the living from the dead when dealing with history and tradition, but let me suggest four criteria. In the first place, if we are to take seriously what has been handed over to us through the centuries, some sense of fidelity and gratitude toward the past would seem to be a preliminary necessity. There are times when respect for the past can become strained, and there are too many times and eras that can only be remembered with shame and remorse. The verdict attributed to Henry Ford that "history is bunk" was a brave, if naïve, defiance of convention on the eve of America's industrial revolution. Sister Corita, during the student protests of the '60s and '70s, liked to repeat the slogan "Damn everything but the circus." And Francis Fukuyama's widely discussed article "The End of History" (*National Interest*, Summer 1989) predicted the "perpetual caretaking of the museum of human history."

But it is cavalier to think we can dismiss the traditions of the past as if we were given superior intellectual and moral insight. There is something arrogant in praising the new at the expense of the past. In any case, so far as biblical research, doctrinal definition, and interpretation of church history are concerned, decisive reinvigoration of the tradition has come by studying the past, not by ignoring it. The Reformers appealed to scripture and the apostolic witness of the early church. Vatican II released the living spirit behind the older Tridentine (1545–1563) formulas.

In both instances a decision about living tradition and dead traditionalism was made.

But, in the second place, fidelity to the past also involves critical scrutiny of the historical sources on which the tradition is based. We no longer teach the allegorical method of biblical exposition, and we have a better knowledge of the development and provenance of the books of the Bible and of the social and political background of the early church—all due to advances in critical scholarship. Our problem today is not ignorance about the past but a virtual glut of scholarly information made available by various electronic retrieval library systems. Critical scrutiny directed toward this vast contemporary scriptorium is required if we are to distinguish what is worth retrieving and what should be allowed to gather dust in the archives of the past.

A third criterion in this discerning process is the contextual situation in which we find ourselves. With some imagination, we can put ourselves back into New Testament times, the Middle Ages, and so on. But our concerns today can be quite different from former times, and it becomes imperative for us to relate the tradition to our own current situation. Not everything in the Bible or church history or theology comes to us today with the same impact or sense of relevancy as formerly. That doesn't necessarily mean we are better or brighter, but if the gospel is to speak to us today, it must be in contexts and associations that seem pertinent and challenging. This criterion is somewhat ambivalent because the temptation to think that we know best what is relevant can be a deceptive trap. What is essential for "us" may not be of any significance whatever for "them." The contextual criterion doesn't imply uniformity, but it forces us to define and articulate what is most important at this moment, in this place, and for this reason.

A fourth criterion for evaluating the traditions of the past concerns fresh discoveries and disclosures about the past. Two current examples illustrate this possibility: the vast, newly documented resources for the black religious experience, especially in the days of slavery, and the equally weighty documentation about the importance of women in a religious history that has been written mostly by men about men. In these two cases, as perhaps in others, tradition must be rewritten, reevaluated, and re-visioned.

III

To carry the flame, not the ashes, implies a refining process that puts aside what is no longer of essential value in order to clarify and simplify what is basic and necessary. In theology, preaching, and religious writing, this refining process is both selective and revisionary. From the cumulative data bank of tradition, we must choose what seems most significant for contemporary concerns, and this also involves a revision of what has gone before. Not everything can be included, whether in a sermon or an essay or a term paper, and there are few, if any, systematizers today who would dare to construct an all-inclusive doctrinal theology.

We must guard against an overly romantic view of carrying on the flame, as if doing so were an easy assignment. There are at least three sobering reservations about theological torchbearing we need to keep in mind. In the first place, the theological task is not only selective and revisionary, it is also necessarily tentative. No one who writes an article or prepares a sermon ever feels that everything has been said and said properly. Theology by its very nature is tentative and, in a sense, always unfinished. Artists, musicians, and poets know this instinctively, and they learn to live with what we called the refining process, knowing full well that what is done may never really be complete.

Schubert's "Unfinished Symphony" provides an almost perfect example of carrying the flame of beautiful music forward but not to completion. Musicologists are not in agreement as to why Franz Schubert left his symphony No. 8 in B Minor unfinished. Maurice Brown, in his article in Grove's *Dictionary of Music and Musicians,* thinks the reason "may lie in psychological factors" aggravated by a severe case of syphilis which left him "desperately ill." If that is indeed the case such a situation emphasizes the precariousness and tentativeness of the human spirit, even in the inspiration of a genius.

In the religious field, most of the current trends—liberation, feminist, black, narrative, and process theology—are very much still in the early stages of development, since history is reckoned by centuries; the notion of completion or finality for those actually engaged in these areas of work would seem irrelevant, even ludicrous. All such theologies implicitly carry the disclaimer "to be continued."

A second reservation or caution about carrying the flame of truth can be illustrated in our response to the teaching of Jesus, especially as noted earlier in the familiar passages of the Sermon on the Mount. When we read, for example, that the meek shall inherit the earth, or that anger is equivalent to murder, or that looking lustfully is the same as adultery, or that we should turn the other cheek, love our enemies, not be anxious, and on and on—we may marvel at the simplicity and essential truth of such sayings. We may say to ourselves that this simple gospel is so obviously carrying the flame, and not the ashes, that we can readily assent to everything that is being prescribed.

But we must be careful here. Jesus is not laying out a program of moral and religious reductionism. We are, in fact, challenged to "exceed" conventional morality, and we are to be tested by how well we keep the new commandment to love each other as Jesus has loved us. That may sound simple, but it's not easy. It is easier to live according to accepted rules and regulations, such as keeping to the right of the road and stopping at red lights. Rules and regulations provide accepted boundaries, limitations, and restrictions.

The Sermon on the Mount is much more difficult because we are on our own to determine where the boundaries are, what we are supposed to do when there are no rules, and how to apply the ethic of love as Jesus personifies it. We can acknowledge the simple gospel of the Sermon on the Mount and at the same time confess our human frailty, our blurred vision, and our moral inertia. Reinhold Niebuhr's so-called "Serenity Prayer," often quoted and of which an adapted version is the recognized invocation at Alcoholics Anonymous meetings, states the dilemma clearly: "God give us the serenity to accept what cannot be changed. Give us the courage to change what should be changed. Give us wisdom to distinguish one from the other."

A third caution when talking about distinguishing the flame from the ashes emerges from Niebuhr's serenity prayer. The wisdom to distinguish is a gift of God, not a natural or innate talent we possess. The classic Christian faith ascribes the power of discerning the difference between flame and ashes to the work of the Holy Spirit. The Spirit who descended on the multitude at

Pentecost came with "tongues as of fire" (Acts 2:3). In Isaac Watts's beloved hymn, we pray that the Spirit may come with "quickening powers" to "kindle a flame of sacred fire in these cold hearts of ours."

Once again, we must be cautious about romanticizing the Spirit as a kindling flame. Fire burns and destroys as well as lights a torch to see into tomorrow. Our Puritan forebears were threatened with fire and brimstone sermons. Jonathan Edward's famous sermon, "Sinners in the Hands of an Angry God," may seem quaint and even perverse to us today. Not often do we hear words from the pulpit such as these: "That world of misery, that lake of burning brimstone, is extended abroad under you. There is the dreadful pit of the glowing flames of the wrath of God. . . . The God that holds you over the pit of hell, such as one holds a spider, or some loathesome insect, over the fire, abhors you, and is dreadfully provoked."

Today we would find such language and imagery offensive. But we have our own fiery symbols in the threat of a nuclear holocaust, even as the Holocaust of World War II continues to burn in our memories and consciences.

There are two aspects of the divine presence as "a consuming fire": one represents destruction, as symbolized in the ashes of seared bones, frizzled flesh, and leaking fusion plants, and the other is a restorative and redemptive image, like the pillar of fire that by night leads us out of darkness and bondage.

In 1943, two years before Hiroshima and the atom bomb, T. S. Eliot put the contrast between the flame of the Spirit and the fire of the world's destruction into memorable lines:

> The dove descending breaks the air
> With flame of incandescent terror
> Of which the tongues declare
> The one discharge from sin and error.
> The only hope, or else despair
> Lies in the choice of pyre or pyre—
> To be redeemed from fire by fire.
>
> "Little Gidding"
> *(Four Quartets,* p. 37)

EIGHT

The Gospel of Grace

Some words in the biblical and theological vocabulary tend to fade in and out of favor for various reasons of time and context. "Creation," for example, was once not so prominent as it is today. The Christocentric emphasis of Karl Barth's theology and the whole neo-orthodox tradition tended to take creation for granted in order to hurry on to the person and work of Jesus Christ. Today, a new concern for creation arises out our ecological crisis, on the one hand, and out of new interpretations of the nature and relation of male and female, on the other hand.

A few words that in previous times carried significant theological weight have all but disappeared. We do not read or hear much about providence, adoption, calling, sanctification, or assurance, to say nothing of predestination and reprobation. These were basic concepts in the Protestant Reformation vocabulary; they correspond, in some measure, with a more relaxed attitude among Catholics toward indulgences, purgatory, and insistence on Latin as the prescribed language for the Mass. Part of the problem of studying theology today, or for that matter preaching from a pulpit every week, is that the religious vocabulary keeps changing.

Some words hang on under new definitions. "Regeneration" now means to be "born again," which is what the word itself suggests. We don't use "salvation" very often, but theologians like to talk about the "salvific" work of God, which sounds more sophisticated. Freedom gets translated into "liberation," and Tillich spoke of sin as "estrangement" and justification as "acceptance." "Thees" and "thous" have long ago disappeared from liturgical forms, new versions of the Bible try to modernize obsolete terms, and many today prefer "Creator, Redeemer,

63

Sanctifier" to the traditional trinitarian names of Father, Son, and Holy Spirit.

Changes in religious vocabulary serve as an excellent barometer for gauging the theological climate of the times. In some ways, we are today more sensitive to the shades of meaning conveyed by the words we use even if, at the same time, we seem to become less literate and articulate. As a sort of test case for these random reflections, let us take the word "grace" and see what it once meant and what it means today.

I

The technical linguistic details for the word "grace" and its various cognates can be found in any good Bible dictionary or encyclopedia. The Hebrew equivalents, *hen* and *hesed,* and the Greek *charis* are translated in English versions by a wide range of words and expressions, such as mercy, favor, steadfast love, loyalty, loving-kindness.

The Greek word for "grace," *charis,* appears in the words "eucharist," "charismatic," and "charisms" (the gifts of the Spirit, cf. Rom. 12:6–8; Eph. 4:11; 1 Cor. 12:8–10; 28–30; 13:1–3; 14:6, 26). "Grace" initiates the sequence of the Apostolic Benediction, "The grace of the Lord Jesus Christ and the love of God and the fellowship of the Holy Spirit be with you all" (2 Cor. 13:14); this is also the sequence of the new Presbyterian "Brief Statement of Faith" (1990). The word "grace" also appears frequently in the Pauline letters as a salutation or postscript.

"The Three Graces" (charity, beauty, love, among other interpretations) date back to classical antiquity and suggest our modern notion of being "gracious," that is, cordial, affable, genial, or sociable. This usage has little to do with the biblical vocabulary, nor do such expressions as "Your Grace" (to an archbishop or a duke), a "grace note" in music, or a "grace period" before making a premium payment, and dozens of other examples that can be found in *The Compact Edition of the Oxford English Dictionary* and elsewhere.

To move closer to the meaning of "grace," as found in the New Testament and as codified and structured in the development of Christian doctrine, we can begin with Augustine, the greatest of the early church theologians, who was given the honorific title of *Doctor Gratia*. Of his voluminous works, several carried the word "grace" in the title, including *On Nature and Grace, On the Grace of Christ and on Original Sin, On Grace and Free Will,* and *On Rebuke and Grace,* as well as several treatises against the Pelagian heresy, which focused primarily upon the difference between grace as God's gift and human free will as necessary for accepting God's grace.

The essence of the Augustinian definition of grace comes directly from the Pauline insistence that, since we are all sinners, God comes to us in Jesus Christ to redeem and save, not because there is anything in us deserving of this divine condescension but only because of God's merciful initiative. Such texts as the following provided Augustine with biblical warrant for stressing God's outgoing and freely given grace without regard for human merit or worth:

> Since all have sinned and fall short of the glory of God, they are justified by his grace as a gift, through the redemption which is in Christ Jesus.
>
> (Rom. 3:23–24)

> God, who is rich in mercy, out of the great love with which he loved us, even when we were dead through our trespasses, made us alive together with Christ (by grace you have been saved). . . . This is not your own doing, it is the gift of God.
>
> (Eph. 2:4–5, 8)

> God, who saved us and called us with a holy calling, not in virtue of our works but in virtue of his own purpose and the grace which he gave us in Christ Jesus.
>
> (2 Tim. 1:8–9)

Such texts provide evidence for viewing God's ready acceptance of sinful humanity not only for Augustine in the early church but for Luther and Calvin in the Reformation, for the Puritans and Jonathan Edwards in early America, and for Barth and Niebuhr in more recent times. Lengthy disputes and angry arguments often set law against gospel, Protestant justification by faith against the Catholic sacramental system, Arminianism against Calvinism, and on and on.

The friction between these opposites has diminished in current theological discussion and, for many, the whole divisive dispute now seems obsolete and irrelevant. But important theological issues were at stake, and the gospel of grace must always defend itself against the charge that emphasis on God's initiative leads to a quietism that precludes human activity on behalf of social justice.

II

It must be admitted that there has always been a quietistic strain in Christian thought and history. Desert recluses such as Jerome (342–420), the medieval anchoress Julian of Norwich (1342–1423), the German Lutheran pietists Philip Jacob Spener (1635–1705) and August Hermann Francke (1663–1727), separatist communities such as Oneida, New Harmony, the Shakers, and the Amish, even Thomas Merton (1915–1968), who not only retreated to a Trappist monastery but had to construct a hidden lean-to in order to escape from prying visitors—all of these and many others remind us that the gospel of grace can be interpreted as reason for retreating from the world. If God does everything for us without regard to human worth or deserving, many would take this to imply an otherworldly life-style and would so interpret Paul's injunction to be in but not of this world (cf. Rom. 12:2).

Such deliberate withdrawal from the world, while appealing to some, would seem to others to deny human freedom and to avoid the possibility of working for a better and more just society. Quietism, in whatever form, runs counter to what has often been called American pragmatism. The Social Gospel that Walter Rauschenbusch advocated just before World War I gave articulate and compelling expression to the liberal and activist passion for doing something rather than seeking refuge in sanctuaries to pray and meditate.

A poignant illustration of this dilemma between faith and works (or faith as grace and faith at work) will be known to those who have seen the film *Witness*. Harrison Ford (*Raiders of the Lost Ark, Return of the Jedi, Star Wars* and others) plays a Philadelphia inner-city cop, involved in the violence of drug traffic, who is forced to protect a young Amish boy, witness to a murder. When the cop must hide out in a Lancaster County Amish community, two cultures come into collision: the peaceful, plain-style Amish, who disdain most modern conveniences, and the cop with a gun, who represents law and order yet goes around bashing people and ends up in a shoot-out in the grainery silo of the barn. He and the young mother of the Amish boy share a romantic attraction, but each knows that there is no future to this, and the cop heads back to Philadelphia while the young woman and her son return to their own community. So, the audience, in a sense, is a witness to two ways of life that move along parallel lines but hardly intersect. The movie, of course, solves nothing and doesn't promote one culture over the other. If the audience were asked to choose sides, chances are that neither culture would get many votes.

But it is not constructive to charge the gospel of grace with otherworldly quietism. Even the Amish, who by conviction do not get involved in social justice issues as generally understood, have their own commitment to their own people and community.

III

The first implication of the gospel of grace is that grace should prompt gratitude and thanksgiving. Wherever in the Bible God's favor and faithfulness are disclosed, there also we are made aware of a gift for which we give thanks. This awareness is not of our own doing but is itself a gift for which we should praise God. "By grace you have been saved through faith; and this is not your own doing, it is the gift of God" (Eph. 2:8).

So, we give thanks to God for the gift of daily bread when we say grace at mealtime, and the Eucharist is a thanksgiving for God's gift in Jesus Christ. Giving and receiving, thanks and praise—these are the reciprocal components of any biblical theology. The Heidelberg Catechism of 1563, among its many excellences, uses the grace-gratitude formula for its basic structure. The first question asks, "What is your only comfort, in life and in death?" And the answer, in part, states, "That I belong . . . not to myself but to my faithful Savior, Jesus Christ." And then the second question asks, "How many things must you know that you may live and die in the blessedness of this comfort?" And the answer declares, "Three. First, the greatness of my sin and wretchedness. Second, how I am freed from all my sins and their wretched consequences. Third, what gratitude I owe to God for such redemption."

The major seasons of the Christian year remind us throughout the year, and year after year, of the grace-gratitude equation. At Christmas, "the wonderous gift is given," and we respond with carols of praise that God has come down to earth, and we give gifts to family and friends. At Eastertide, we celebrate the gift of eternal life and sing with angels and archangels, "Alleluia! Alleluia!" At Pentecost, we remember the gift of the Spirit that came upon the disorganized group of early Christians, when they began to "speak" together in a new language, having "all things in common" and "praising God" (cf. Acts 2:4, 44, 47).

The gratitude side of the gospel of grace represents the human response to God's gift. This is the point at which, in German, we could play around with the words *Gabe* (gift) and *Aufgabe* (task). But in any language the receiving of God's grace in Jesus Christ produces grateful commitment, a cause-and-effect sequence experienced by those who have left first-person accounts of conversion. But it also characterizes many individuals who, for whatever reason, decide to change the direction of their lives.

Albert Schweitzer is perhaps the most exemplary illustration of recent times. When Schweitzer decided to become a jungle doctor, out of other more obvious options, he was following up on an idea that had long germinated in his mind. "It struck me," he wrote in *Out of My Life and Thought*, "as incomprehensible that I should be allowed to lead such a happy life while I saw so many people around me wrestling with care and suffering. . . . Then one brilliant morning . . . there came to me, as I awoke, the thought that I must not accept this happiness as a matter of course, but must give something in return for it" (p. 102). We may wonder if Schweitzer had been thinking of the text, "Every one to whom much is given, of him will much be required" (Luke 12:48).

A more contemporary example of active gratitude in response to God's grace would be former President Jimmy Carter and his quiet but persistent commitment to Habitat for Humanity's efforts to build homes for the poor and needy in the South and elsewhere. Everyone knows that Jimmy Carter describes himself as a "born again" Christian and that his manual labor is a reflection of his faith. When not hammering and sawing, he still teaches a Sunday School class at his Baptist church in Plains, Georgia.

The Gospel of Grace

Another example, on a much wider scale, is provided by a 1988 survey conducted by the Gallup Organization for the Washington-based *Independent Sector*. The survey "From Belief to Commitment," details the large amounts of money church members donate to charitable causes in their own communities and internationally. Such financial support is described as "dwarfing all funds contributed to and by other voluntary organizations for local human services" (p. iii). Beyond that startling and mostly unpublicized gesture of generosity, the survey also discovered that church buildings in local communities, in addition to being used for worship services and religious education, are open to a large variety of community enterprises, such as Alcoholics Anonymous meetings, soup kitchens, and clothes for the homeless.

There are two additional findings in the Gallup survey worth mentioning. Financial support from church members in terms of percentage of participation comes as much from the poorer congregations as from the more affluent. And secondly, the amount of volunteer social service on the part of church members is incalculable, as every hospital, welfare agency, and even local political headquarters knows very well indeed.

There is an old story about a Quaker who asked a neighbor to accompany her to a Friends' Meeting. After sitting in silence for a long time, the neighbor whispered, "When does the service begin?" The Friend whispered back, "The service begins after the worship."

A second implication of the gospel of grace is that praise, thanksgiving, and gratitude associated with God's free gift come as an afterthought. To put it more accurately, it is the *experience* of God's gift that makes possible and, indeed, necessary a theology of grace. The title of Bunyan's autobiography, *Grace Abounding to the Chief of Sinners* (1666), is an accurate description of his own Christian experience. We can respond to Bonhoeffer's distinction between "cheap grace" and "costly grace," as outlined in *The Cost of Discipleship* (German edition, 1937; English edition, 1949), because we know that for him the Christian faith holds the cross of Christ at the center and that he himself paid the cost of his own life for his faith.

In Robert Fulghum's best-seller, *All I Really Need to Know I Learned in Kindergarten* (1988), the one-time minister reflects that for him "Wisdom was not at the top of the graduate-school mountain, but there in the sandpile at Sunday School" (p. 6). But his simple credo, based on elementary truths and axioms, did not emerge while he was a child but only on reflection, much later.

The last verse of the anonymous hymn, "I Sought the Lord," gives expression to this reflective process:

> I find, I walk, I love, but O the whole of love
>   is but my answer, Lord, to Thee!
> For Thou wert long beforehand with my soul;
>   always Thou lovedst me.

IV

A third implication of the gospel of grace presupposes our common, human finitude and the awareness that what sustains us in life is the gracious presence of the divine and the assurance that "underneath are the everlasting arms" (Deut. 33:27). This realistic and unsentimental perspective ties in with a considerable body of secular wisdom that suggests to win is to lose a little. Let three illustrations from films speak for this aphorism. Sam Goldwyn, the grand old man of the movies, finally received an Academy Award in 1947. After the ceremonies, so it is reported, his wife Frances found him sitting on a couch in their living room, the lights turned off, his head in his hands, softly sobbing to himself as he handled the Oscar.

In the film *Chariots of Fire*, Ben Cross plays Harold Abrahams, a Jewish runner at Cambridge University who knows something about academic anti-Semitism. In the 1924 Olympics, he wins his race and returns to the locker room to cool off. Two other contestants nearby talk about the race, and one says he should go over and congratulate Abrahams. But the other, who sees the victor off by himself with a towel over his head, restrains the well-wisher and says, in effect, "No, leave him alone. Let him have some time to himself." F. Scott Fitzgerald once said, "Show me a hero, and I will write you a tragedy."

After the last episode in the popular Masterpiece Theatre production of *The Jewel in the Crown* (1984), the television audience was treated to several interviews with some of the cast. One of the questioners asked Tim Piggott-Smith, who played the stiff-lipped Colonel Merrick, why there were so many loose ends after fourteen chapters. He replied that when the British left India, some things changed for the better, but that India's religious and political divisions remained and further violence soon broke out. Beyond that, the actor added that all the characters in the play were themselves divided in their loyalties, and their own futures seemed unsure and unpredictable.

Those who affirm the gospel of grace have an instinctive sympathy with all such illustrations of human finitude. After all, the Bible is full of characters who, on the side of faith, know what it means to both win and lose. Moses, after leading the children of Israel out of their Egyptian bondage, is not permitted to enter the promised land but must be content to view it from afar. Elijah must pass the prophetic mantle on to Elisha. Tamar, who appears in Matthew's genealogy of Jesus, has to pose as a prostitute to seduce her father-in-law into facing the truth. Simeon does not live to see the salvation he glimpses in the infant Christ child, and he predicts that "a sword will pierce" Mary's heart. Peter confesses that Jesus is the Messiah and then later denies that he ever knew him. Stephen, who worked at the apostolic soup kitchen, distributing food to widows, is granted a vision of the risen Lord, and then is stoned to death, as Paul, before his Damascus experience, looks on.

The gospel of grace is not the solution to all problems, personal or social. It can and often has been misconstrued and distorted. But it remains one sure way to define the simple gospel. In 1952, two important events marked the prolific and influential career of Reinhold Niebuhr. It was the year he published *The Irony of American History,* a book that brought forth vigorous criticism from political and social liberals for what they took to be his passive acquiescence to divine determination. It was also the year that he suffered a stroke that did not immobilize him but initiated a decline until his death in 1971.

While at the Institute for Advanced Study at Princeton in 1958, Niebuhr told his friend, Elmer G. Homrighausen, "Homey, I'm all right except for this damn, frail, human body." Against that background, and perhaps in ominous anticipation, he wrote these typically aphoristic lines:

Nothing that is worth doing can be achieved in our lifetime; therefore we must be saved by hope. Nothing that is true or beautiful makes complete sense in any immediate context of history; therefore we must be saved by faith. Nothing we do, however virtuous, can be accomplished alone; therefore we must be saved by love. No virtuous act is quite as virtuous from the standpoint of our friend or foe as it is from our standpoint. Therefore, we must be saved by the final form of love which is forgiveness.

The Irony of American History (p. 63)

That, after all these years, is as good a definition of the gospel of grace as we are ever likely to get. Was there, we may imagine, not only a premonition of life's finite limitations in these words but also a personal resonance with the apostle Paul, who prayed three times that his "thorn in the flesh" be removed? The answer to his prayers? "My grace is sufficient for you, for my power is made perfect in weakness" (2 Cor. 12:7–9).

Euagelio (that we cal gospel) is a
greke worde, and signyfyth good, mery,
glad and joyfull tydings, that maketh a
mannes hert glad, and maketh him synge,
daunce and leepe for ioye.

William Tyndale, *Prologue
to the New Testament*, 1525

Index

73